I0518642

True Mercy Has Teeth
A Catholic Journey to Forgiveness and Healing

Fr. Todd Petersen

MERCY WITH TEETH
PRESS

Disclaimer:
Note to the Reader
While this book touches on emotional and psychological wounds, it is not a substitute for professional counseling or therapy. I write as a priest and fellow pilgrim, drawing from Scripture, Catholic teaching, and personal experience. If you are struggling with trauma, depression, or mental health issues, please consider speaking with a qualified therapist or counselor, especially one who respects your faith journey. Healing often takes a team - and God works through many hands.

Copyright © 2025 Fr. Todd Petersen
All rights reserved.

No part of this publication may be reproduced, stored in a retrieval system, or transmitted in any form or by any means - electronic, mechanical, photocopy, recording, or otherwise - without the prior written permission of the author, except in the case of brief quotations embodied in critical articles or reviews.

Unless otherwise noted, Scripture quotations are taken from the New American Bible - Revised Edition.
The Catechism of the Catholic Church is quoted with gratitude and respect for its public role in the life of the Church.

This book is a work of non-fiction. Every effort has been made to maintain accuracy and truth.

Printed in the United States of America

ISBN: Soft Cover 979-8-9994781-0-8
        Hard Cover 979-8-9994781-2-2
        Kindle 979-8-9994781-1-5
First Edition
Mercy With Teeth Press
www.MercyWithTeeth.com

Table of Contents

Forward:

Rev. Todd Petersen, a Catholic priest, has written a very helpful book on forgiveness and healing for survivors of abuse, whether that be physical, or sexual, or psychological abuse. In his book, Fr. Petersen draws on his own personal experience of psychological abuse by a parent, as well as his rich pastoral experience as a priest. In other words, he is a survivor himself, who has ministered to survivors.

The story begins at the beginning of Scripture with the story of the Creation and Fall. The Fall, instigated by Satan, introduces evil into the world. The book speaks of the consequences of the evil of abuse. A survivor is apt to feel fear, anger, shame, anxiety, depression, used, manipulated, vengeful, and so many other consequences. In page after page Fr. Petersen shows how the merciful heart of Jesus brings good out of the evil of sin and its consequences and makes all things new. Consequently, Christ brings hope to survivors. With Christ, their lives are not over.

Fr. Petersen outlines how a life in Christ, the Good Shepherd, will "make new" the survivors by helping them to forgive the other and to heal the deep wounds brought about by the evil they have suffered. The book integrates the fountains of the grace of Christ, including prayer, the Sacraments, the Scriptures, the teaching of the Church (the *Catechism*), the beatitudes, the virtues, and much more. It is grace that helps to bring about forgiveness and healing.

Fr. Petersen has done a service to the Church, especially for the survivors of abuse. In addition to the above, Fr. Petersen provides an appendix with many prayers and resources. The book is readable and practical. It is honest. No whitewashing or attempts to hide the truth here. This is a book with teeth.

Most Reverend John M. LeVoir
Bishop Emeritus of New Ulm

Thank you:

Thank you, first, to the holy and wise spiritual directors and counselors who have walked with me and many others.

Thank you to the Most Reverend Chad Zielinski, Bishop of New Ulm, who has supported this project.

Thank you to Bishop LeVoir, Bishop Emeritus of the Diocese of New Ulm, whose wisdom helped me in a time of crisis, modeled healing and reconciliation, and who has also supported this project. He has written the Forward that you just read.

Thank you to the many parishioners from many of the parishes I have served who have allowed me to serve them, and who have taught me so much.

Thank you to Christopher Hjelmberg, who lovingly edited this book, pulling me into conciseness to help you, the reader.

Thank you to my family, especially my sisters and my mother's extended family. You have shown what family ought to be.

In memory of my mom, my grandparents, and all those who were "Jesus with flesh on," who have passed.

Introduction: What's the Matter

> "The divine fatherhood is the source of human
> fatherhood; this is the foundation of the honor owed
> to parents. The respect of children, whether minors
> or adults, for their father and mother is nourished by
> the natural affection born of the bond uniting them.
> It is required by God's commandment."
>
> – Catechism of the Catholic Church, ¶2214

To say I had a strained relationship with my father would be a vast understatement. His expectations of me were unspoken, inconsistent, and unreasonable. My life—its milestones, joys, hardships—was seemingly an afterthought.

About a month after my high school graduation (a graduation my father was late for) my mother reached her breaking point. She had information of his having *another* affair. My parents separated and eventually divorced. Through the tribunal process my mother received a Declaration of Nullity (see the Appendix for more on marriage). Whatever relationship I had with my father became even more fractured.

Despite the pain, I still loved him and sought to honor him.

Shortly before Christmas a few months later, I reached out in a spirit of reconciliation. I sent a letter expressing love, sharing the things I respected about him, and honestly admitting I was struggling to forgive him for having an affair. His response was devastating. He called my mother to inform her of his discontent with my letter, mischaracterizing my letter as hateful and arrogant. He told her to tell me that he disowned me. Swayed by his narrative, others pressured me to apologize and beg for his forgiveness. My mother, though well-meaning, often told me that I had to, "...let it go."

Even as the pain of that reality was settling in, I discerned a call to the Priesthood. Despite the hurt and rejection, I invited him to my priestly ordination seven years later. I held onto hope for reconciliation, spending the night sleepless and in prayer over our relationship instead of preparation for the Sacrament of Holy Orders. He arrived five minutes before the Ordination Mass began and left before it ended. He later shared with my mother of his disappointment that I did not take time to talk with him. To be honest, I did not even know he was there until he was gone.

About a year later, I had a face-to-face encounter with him for the first time after I sent the letter seeking reconciliation. Despite all my previous efforts to reconcile, to be a son of whom my father could be proud of, I was met with unjust accusations of disrespect and disobedience. He cursed me, spewed rage, and tore me apart. Suffice to say, this encounter with my father shattered me. I felt numb. The poison of my father's harsh and condemning words lingered. I was drowning in it. I questioned my vocation, my sense of worth, even my identity. Was I as disrespectful as he claimed? Did I dishonor him? Was I unlovable? Was I unworthy of existence? How can I be a priest if that were all true?

It took time to find equilibrium again, to be able to feel genuinely loved by anyone, including God. I felt robotic, like I was going through the motions. Presiding at Mass was painful. How could I be authentic knowing someone felt so ill of me. I loved being a priest, but I had allowed his behavior to poison me. I struggled to forgive - not only him, but myself for letting it happen. If only I had done something. I did not remain in that encounter with my father out of filial piety, I stayed because I still wanted a relationship with my father, something that for me, sadly, will never be possible. I did not know I was ensnared in a pattern of dysfunction - his and mine. I lacked the tools to respond differently.

With the benefit of prayer, time, and healing, I realized he was not a mad dog barking, but was baring his teeth to me merely scared. My father was more like a wounded lone wolf - isolated, incapable of true relationship, at least with me.

I knew I had to forgive - not only his actions, but the apathy, the absence of love. I had to let go of the poison. I had to pray and re-pray through the pain, and I had to ask where Jesus was in it all. I came to understand that the Lord was holding me through it all, that God allowed those moments not to harm me, but to free me. God did not want my heart twisted by pain. He wanted it whole - capable of loving and of being loved. He wanted me to live a more abundant life. And while the image of my father was one of hatred, the Lord showed another more powerful image: He was there, holding me, loving me, smiling at me. It was a smile that did not ignore the evil or pain I endured, but a smile of the

2

invitation to trust in Him, to know that He was offering strength. In it, He showed mercy. A truly toothy mercy, perhaps, as He protected me from what could have been so much worse. If it were not for Him, I do not know what would have happened to me.

Grace held me through those experiences where I not only began to understand the world's evil more deeply, but the depth of God's love and mercy despite it. This understanding eventually gave rise to this book, with my first audience being myself.

I know others have endured worse. Pain is not a contest. Every act of evil - no matter how great or small - is a rupture in the abundant life Jesus came to give. Many people are deeply wounded, some beyond what we can imagine. Physical abuse, emotional betrayal, sexual violence - these are horrors no person should endure.

Evil causes many to question whether God is real, whether He is good, whether He truly loves. Some abandon belief altogether. Others, having never truly faced evil, refuse to acknowledge its presence. Worse, they blame the survivors. They try to silence them. They minimize the trauma. Or worse, they become the perpetrators.

This book is for those who have stared evil in the face - and for those who have not yet recognized it in their midst. It asks a hard question: What is the Christian response to evil and to evildoers? How do those affected by the sin of others forgive and grow in holiness?

We are often trained, implicitly or explicitly, to ignore evil. We are told that others have it worse, so our issues are less. We are encouraged to forgive without addressing harm. We misunderstand Scripture's call to turn the other cheek as a command to ignore the hurt at best, or a demand to remain open to further abuse at worst, to endure anything. We are told that to be merciful is to abandon strength and the hope of justice or accountability.

Yes, Christian charity requires endurance and forgiveness. But charity does not mean passivity. Charity does not allow for toothless justice or false mercy.
This book aims to define that type of mercy and help it be lived. First, we will explore the Catholic theology of evil, looking at morality and the problem of evil in God's grand design. In Part Two, we will explore

a beautiful passage of Scripture, the Good Shepherd narrative, that will help refine our understanding of the Lord's response to evil. Part Three will be an invitation to enter into the pain and brokenness with the Lord, to journey into healing. Part Four will be an invitation to living an abundant life that the Lord promises.

I pray that this book is a testimony of hope in the face of evil. Jesus did not come to make us nice, to cozy up with evil. He came to make us holy. And sometimes, holiness demands that we speak truth, challenge injustice, and protect the vulnerable.

Even when it hurts.
Especially when it hurts.

May this book be a call to recognize, name, and confront evil - not with rage, but with Christ's truth and compassion and mercy. It is about finding and living mercy - but not the kind of mercy that lets evil flourish. It is about mercy with teeth: the kind that sets boundaries, names truth, and defends the dignity of the wounded. The kind Jesus showed. The kind that says, 'no more' - and still forgives.

Part One: The Root of Evil
1. What Is Evil, Really?

> "If God the Father almighty, the Creator of the
> ordered and good world, cares for all his creatures,
> why does evil exist? To this question, as pressing as
> it is unavoidable and as painful as it is mysterious,
> no quick answer will suffice. Only Christian faith as
> a whole constitutes the answer."
>
> – Catechism of the Catholic Church, ¶309

Most of us are aware that evil exists. But few of us reflect deeply on its nature or how we should respond to it - especially as Christians. The Church, through her saints and teachings, has wrestled with this mystery for millennia.

What is "evil"

St. Augustine, followed by St. Thomas Aquinas, taught that evil is not a created thing in itself, but rather a privation - a lack of some good that ought to be present. Evil is a wound, a distortion, a corruption of what was meant to be whole.

There are several kinds of evil. We can speak of physical evil - like disease, disasters, and death. We can speak of metaphysical evil, which refers to natural limitations (a sparrow that cannot fly, for instance). But our purpose here is primarily concerned with moral evil - the kind that results from human or demonic choices. The kind that wounds the soul and the community.

Let us propose the following analogies: A rock cannot see, but that is not evil - it was never meant to see. A child born blind experiences metaphysical evil - it is a tragedy because sight is natural to human beings. A sparrow that cannot fly experiences a form of evil; humans, who are not meant to fly unaided, do not. These distinctions help us grasp what Aquinas meant: evil is the absence or distortion of a good that should be there.

Moral evil arises when a person chooses against the good they were made to pursue, when they do evil or avoid doing good.

In the New Testament Greek, there are several words for "evil."

- *Kakos/kakia* refers to a moral evil or evil disposition - what is inherently wrong, evil in being.
- *Ponēros* describes that which is actively harmful or destructive - evil in action
- *Phaulos* refers to something worthless, failing to achieve its proper end, evil in not fulfilling its proper 'end' or purpose.

All three are relevant when we talk about evildoers. Some people fail to do good, some do evil, and others seem to be evil, so given to it that it seems part of their constitution.

Sin

When the Church talks about sin, it is addressing moral evil. Sin is an offense against God, but not all sin is equally grave. Following the teaching of St. John, the Church distinguishes between mortal and venial sins (1 John 5:17). Mortal sin is deadly - it breaks the life of grace in the soul. Venial sin wounds it, but does not sever our relationship with God, at least not at once.

Think of sin like poison. Some poisons kill instantly, like cyanide. Others harm slowly, like botulism. Mortal sin is spiritual cyanide. Venial sin, when accumulated, can still be deadly over time.

Three conditions must be present for a sin to be mortal:
- Grave matter - a serious violation of God's law.
- Full knowledge - awareness that the action is gravely wrong.
- Deliberate consent - a free choice to commit the act.

There is also the distinction between vincible ignorance (what we could or should have known) and invincible ignorance (what we could not reasonably have known). This is important when considering culpability. Someone who could not have known is less guilty of sin than someone who should have known.

We tend to see morality in black and white, or some areas are a little gray. There are areas of grave matter, the deadly sins of pride, avarice/greed, Acadia/sloth, gluttony, wrath, pride, envy. Certainly, these are to be avoided because they are grave. But the Church desires more than "following the rules." The reality is that the Church teaches these so that we can *live abundantly* by living beyond them in a life of virtue. In the end, so we can live in right relationship with the Lord. The

Cardinal and Theological virtues- prudence, justice, temperance, and fortitude, faith, hope, and charity-become part of your character. Sin becomes unthinkable because we do not wish to hurt our relationship with the Lord. Our Christian life is about following Jesus Christ as a disciple, out of love, not fear and not just following rules. It is about following Jesus.

Why these distinctions matter
Understanding these all distinctions of types of evil, culpability and sin allows us to confront evil without condemning the person. It offers a place for truth, justice, and ultimately - conversion.

But to fully understand the Church's response to evil, we must look at the larger story: Salvation History.

For Reflection:
- How do I usually think about evil?
- When thinking of moral evil, how does it help to consider if it is an inherent evil, an evil act, or a failure to do what was good?
- How do I view morality? Is it all black and white? How much gray? Is it a matter of rules, or about relationship?
- Read Psalm 36

2. The Big Picture: Salvation History and The Reality of Evil

> Creation is the foundation of "all God's saving
> plans," the "beginning of the history of salvation"
> that culminates in Christ. Conversely, the mystery of
> Christ casts conclusive light on the mystery of
> creation and reveals the end for which "in the
> beginning God created the heavens and the earth":
> from the beginning, God envisaged the glory of the
> new creation in Christ.
>
> – Catechism of the Catholic Church, ¶280

To properly respond to evil, we must understand where it fits within God's plan. Evil is not the whole story. It has a beginning - and it has an end. God allows evil but is not the cause. In His permissive will, He allows it to bring about a greater good. The narrative of salvation history helps us see this arc.

Dr. Christopher Thompson, a professor of Moral Theology at the University of St. Thomas, provided a succinct model for this grand story. In his introductory courses to morality, both at an undergraduate and our graduate level, he taught a seven-stage structure that situates morality within the larger context of divine history. Whenever any student had a too rosy view of humanity or failed to recognize original sin or its effects, he would gently remind the class that the Fall is Chapter Two. When viewed this way, evil is not ignored but placed in its proper place: a deviation to which God responds with justice, mercy, and ultimately, redemption.

While seven "chapters" in this great Story of Salvation, there are two ways of see its structure. We can see that Christ's Resurrection begins a new Creation and leads to union with God for eternity, in a parallel structure. But there is also a chiasm - a literary pattern with a mirrored structure that emphasizes a pivotal point. As each chapter mirrors another, we might see something else: the Law is the dwelling of the Holy Spirit, the Fall is the lifting up of humanity in the Final Judgment, and Eternal Life is now greater than creation itself. The center of both patterns, not coincidentally, is Christ an His redemption.

To help visualize these structures:
Parallel Structure:

Creation	←→	The Church The Holy Spirit
The Fall	←→	Final Judgment
The Law & Prophets	←→	Eternal Life

Starting over: Christ's Redemption

This Pattern shows that God has created and recreated. And He will bring all things to Himself.

Chiastic Structure:
A. Creation
　　B. The Fall
　　　　C. The Law and the Prophets
　　　　　　X. Christ's Redemption (The Turning Point)
　　　　C•. The Church and Indwelling of the Spirit
　　B•. Final Judgment
A•. Eternal Life

This pattern reveals that the goal is not merely restoration, but something greater than what was lost. God does not only restore Eden, but He also brings us home to eternal union with Him.

Chapter 1: Creation

God created everything in love. Humanity, made in His image, was the crown of that creation. In the first chapters of Genesis, we encounter a world marked by peace and harmony. Humans enjoyed intimacy with God, with one another, and with themselves. Adam and Eve were "naked and unashamed" - a symbol of complete trust and unity.

God provided for them, placing them in a garden filled with beauty and sustenance. He gave only one command: do not eat from the Tree of the Knowledge of Good and Evil. They were not explicitly forbidden from partaking of the Tree of Life. Everything was properly ordered to its purpose - what theologians call original justice. They were at home.
In this original state, man knew God, loved Him, and lived in communion with creation.

Chapter 2: The Fall

This harmony was short-lived. In Genesis 3, the serpent - cunning and deceitful - tempted Eve. He questioned God's motives, accused Him of jealousy, and promised that disobedience would bring enlightenment. "You will not surely die," he lied. He told half-truths, the most dangerous kind of deception.

Eve looked at the fruit. She saw that it was good for food (lust of the flesh), pleasing to the eye (lust of the eyes), and desirable for wisdom (pride of life). Adam, standing silently nearby, failed to protect or intervene. He too took and ate. Sin entered the world.

With their disobedience came shame, blame, and separation. They hid from each other and from God. They blamed others - Adam blamed Eve; Eve blamed the serpent. In that single act, the seeds of all sin were planted: disobedience, pride, fear, shame, and alienation.

Death entered - not only physical death, but spiritual death: the rupture of communion with God, the loss of their home.

Though He cast them from the garden, God did not abandon them. He promised redemption in Genesis 3:15 - the Protoevangelium, the first Gospel: one would come from the woman who would crush the serpent's head.

The effects of the Fall endure. The Church Fathers named four:
- Death - separation of soul and body.
- Disease or suffering - physical and emotional pain.
- Darkened intellect - difficulty discerning truth.
- Desire to sin or Concupiscence - the inclination toward sin.

These wounds mark all of humanity. We are not punished for Adam's sin *per se*, but we inherit the brokenness it caused. This is the doctrine of Original Sin - the broken state into which we are all born.

Chapter 3: The Law and the Prophets

Even before the moment of the Fall, God began His work of redemption. The rest of the Old Testament tells this story: humanity's sin, God's call, their return, and the cycle repeating.

Cain kills Abel. Humanity grows corrupt. A flood purifies the earth, but sin remains. God calls Abraham, Isaac, and Jacob. He leads their descendants out of slavery in Egypt through Moses. He gives them the Law - but even in the desert, they rebel.

He gives them the Promised Land - but they forget Him. Judges rise to lead, but the people demand a king. Some kings are faithful; many are not. Prophets speak God's word - sometimes heard, often rejected.

Still, God continued to prepare the world for a Savior.

Chapter 4: Christ's Redemption

In the fullness of time, God sent His Son (Gal. 4:4). Jesus Christ, fully divine and fully human, entered the world not merely to teach or to heal - but to redeem.

The Incarnation, Jesus taking on flesh, was not a Plan B. From the beginning, God knew humanity would fall. The Cross was not an accident - it was the _centerpiece_ of His plan.

Christ's life, death, and resurrection are the turning point of history. He offered His life as a sacrifice to conquer sin and death. Every evil chapter, every wound, every sin was taken to the Cross.
Jesus did not come to erase the pain of the world, but to transform it. In Him, evil is not only acknowledged - it is defeated.

Chapter 5: The Church and the Indwelling of the Spirit

The story of salvation did not end at the resurrection. In many ways, it began again.

Jesus ascended into heaven, but He did not leave us orphans. At Pentecost, the Holy Spirit descended on the apostles and disciples, including the Blessed Virgin Mary, empowering the Church to proclaim the Gospel to the ends of the earth. This moment, when the Spirit hovered - not over formless waters, as in Genesis - but over the gathered Church, marked a new creation.

This chapter is still unfolding. We live in the era of the Church - the Body of Christ continuing His mission on earth. Through the sacraments, the Church dispenses grace. Through her teaching, she proclaims truth. Through her witness, she confronts sin and evil. Evil is being unraveled and conquered, though the War is already won.

The Church is holy because her Head is Christ and she is animated by the Holy Spirit. Yet she is always in need of purification because her members - bishops, priests, religious, and laity - remain human and prone to sin. Concupiscence lingers. We fall short. We fail. But the Church herself will never fall away from Christ. As the Second Vatican Council taught, "The Church... clasping sinners to her bosom, at once holy and always in need of purification, follows constantly the path of penance and renewal" (*Lumen Gentium*, 8). Through the abiding presence of the Holy Spirit, she remains the Bride of Christ and the vessel of His mercy - even when some of her members distort that image. She is holy and being made holy, all at once - because Christ is faithful, even when we are not.

This chapter in the chiastic structure mirrors the time of the Law and the Prophets. Then, God spoke through judges and prophets. Now, He speaks through His Spirit, alive in the Church. We have been given the sacraments - visible signs of invisible grace - to sustain us in holiness.

In the parallel structure, this chapter reflects a new creation. As the Spirit hovered over the waters in Genesis, so now He fills the Church with life and direction.

Chapter 6: Christ's Return and Judgment

One day, Christ will return. We do not know the hour or the day, but the promise is sure. At His return, He will judge the living and the dead.

All will rise - body and soul reunited - and stand before the Lord. This is not metaphorical. It is the culmination of our human story.

For the faithful, resurrection brings glory, and four important gifts of a glorified human:
- Impassibility - no more suffering or corruption.
- Agility - perfect harmony between soul and body.
- Subtlety - no longer bound by the laws of nature, moving with a single thought.
- Clarity - shining with divine light.

For the unrepentant, resurrection is not glory but condemnation. God reveals to them their destiny apart from Him. Separation from God is no longer only spiritual - it becomes complete and eternal. They are separated from the Source of Life.

God does not arbitrarily condemn. He confirms the choices we made with our lives. As CS Lewis wrote in *The Great Divorce*, "There are only two kinds of people in the end: those who say to God, 'Thy will be done,' and those to whom God says, in the end, 'Thy will be done.'"

This chapter mirrors and parallels the Fall in both structures. Even as the Fall introduced separation and death, the Final Judgment brings restoration or permanent separation, depending on one's response to grace.

There is profound hope here. Until this moment, the offer of mercy stands. But once we reach this chapter, there are no more revisions to our story.

Chapter 7: Eternal Life

Eternity is not a continuation of time - it is its fulfillment.

For those who love God, eternal life is perfect communion: seeing Him face-to-face, participating in the Beatific Vision, resting in joy that never ends. We will be more than restored - we will be glorified, beyond even what Adam and Eve experienced in Eden. There, they will find a true home for all eternity.

For those who reject God, eternity is also permanent - but marked by absence. Hell is not only fire and brimstone, worse, it is the reality of eternal separation from the Source of life and joy. And the condemned souls burn with hatred.

God does not force us into heaven. Love cannot be coerced. If someone persistently chooses evil, persists in rejecting God and others, then God honors that freedom - even though it breaks His heart.

This chapter mirrors Creation in chiastic structure. But it is not a return to Eden - it is something greater. We are not simply restored; we are transformed. In eternity, God once again looks at His people and says, "It is good." In the parallel structure, it is paired with the Law and the prophets, but now God is with His people for eternity, and they will never depart from Him.

The final chapters - Final Judgment and Eternal Life - are perhaps the most difficult for many to accept. We live in a culture that idolizes tolerance and avoids talk of consequences. It pretends that all is made right, that nothing is sinful because all is redeemed. All go to heaven, to be with a god who demands nothing. But Christ speaks clearly about hell, judgment, and the need for conversion. To deny these is not to be compassionate - it is to be dishonest.

The Gospel is good news. But it is only truly good if our Savior rescues us from something real. Evil exists. Sin still happens. Judgment awaits. But so does mercy - and eternal joy. The truly Good News is that we are invited into an eternal union with Him.

Your Story Is Part of the Great Story God Is Telling

The beautiful part of the seven chapters of salvation history is that it provides a framework for our individual lives. We are born, created children of God, born with original sin and in separation from the Father, who loves us. We sin, and at some point, we recognize a call from God. We encounter Christ, some of us in a dramatic and powerful way, others through more ordinary activities, such as the Sacraments or through a solid example of faithful parents, for example. No matter what, though, there will be a point in which Christ becomes central in our life if we want to grow in holiness. Then we live with Him, with the Holy Spirit, seeking to do God's will and coming back to God's mercy when we sin. We are in Chapter Five, and it is a time of profound hope, no matter what is going on, because we are alive and we are able to choose new. We can change. We can repent. We can grow. We can adapt. We can be transformed. While we have breath, and in the freedom permitted to us by God, we have a say in the telling of our story.

But then, we will die. This is the reality of our lives. When we do, we enter into the Last Four Things: Death, Judgment, Heaven, and Hell. Those who die in grace, prepared fully to be with the Lord, being completely detached from sin and concupiscence, enter into Heavenly Joy. They join the great cloud of witnesses- the angels and Saints- in the eternal song of praise. Their story is written and complete, and then they live in the story that does not end.

Those who die in sin, refusing to accept God's grace, go to another state, as already mentioned. They go to the place of eternal separation, to the Hell that has been prepared for Satan and all the Fallen angels, the demons. Their torture begins, and their story is complete, but lived out for eternity in that place of torture.

But what happens to those who die in grace, but still have attachment to sin, or have yet to face the consequences of their sins? They are not ready to enter into eternal joy as their hearts are divided. And while not completely given to the Lord, they do love Him and tried to do God's will. It would seem cruel for the Lord to condemn them to Hell. Not able to enter heaven, not deserving of hell. Here is where God shows mercy with teeth. As the Catholic Church teaches, God grants a state of purification for those who need it, a state of purgation and joyful suffering. We call this Purgatory. There, the soul's disordered attachments are purged away, as concupiscence is finally defeated and the soul loves in the proper order of God above all else. It is there that whatever temporal effects of sin can be satisfied, and right relationship can be restored.

Think of this temporal punishment like this. If I would break a window, I can be sorry. My sorrow does not repair the window. It remains broken. You could ask me to repair it myself, taking it out and to a professional or figuring it out on my own. You could get it fixed and ask me to either work it off or pay for it. Or you might simply forgive it, but you would still need to have it repaired. Sin is like that. Jesus already paid the debt, but we need to accept that grace and seek to repair the damage done. This is the beauty of the gift of penance, especially in the Sacrament of Reconciliation. It recognizes that we owe God a debt we cannot repay, and therefore He paid it. But penance is that we do something to help receive and grow in holiness. And when we do, we are fully reconciled to the God who waits for us to return home like the Lost Son.

In Purgatory, these acts come in ways known to God alone, but they are His mercies. Our sin has consequences, and God's mercy with teeth helps us to make repartition.

But Purgatory will end, mercifully. In the fullness of time, when the soul is purified and ready, God brings the person to heaven.

When Christ comes again, each will be entered in the Final Judgment, and eternity is settled. We will either be with God for eternity or be eternally separated from Him. And while still have breath, we are in control of where we will end. Our story is still being written, and where we end in the closing chapter is ours to decide. Either we seek God, accept His grace, seek His forgiveness, make reparation as needed, and seek to live a life of holiness, and we will be home. Or we chose ourselves, our own wants and desires, and chose against the God of Love, and separated from Him who loved us so.

For Reflection:
- Looking at the seven chapters of salvation history, how does this help give hope or peace when facing sin and evil?
- How do I live the redemption of Christ and the dwelling of the Holy Spirit?
- Where do I want my story to end?
- How is the very teaching of salvation an example of God's mercy and love
- Read Genesis 3

3. Inside the Heart: Why We Choose to Do Evil

> "The 'mastery' over the world that God offered man
> from the beginning was realized above all within
> man himself: mastery of self. The first man was
> unimpaired and ordered in his whole being because
> he was free from the triple concupiscence that
> subjugates him to the pleasures of the senses,
> covetousness for earthly goods, and self-assertion,
> contrary to the dictates of reason."
>
> – Catechism of the Catholic Church, ¶377

People do not choose evil for evil's sake - not knowingly anyway. This may seem hard to believe, especially when confronted with deliberate acts of cruelty or manipulation. But at the root of most human evil is not a desire to do wrong, but a mistaken grasping at what seems good.

We are made to seek the good. But because of original sin, our vision is clouded, our judgment skewed. We are often confused about what the good is, or how best to pursue it. In many cases, people choose evil because they perceive some distorted benefit - pleasure, control, safety, affirmation. Even those who commit terrible harm often believe they are protecting themselves or achieving justice.

Take addiction, for example. An addict does not wake up seeking self-destruction. They seek relief, escape, or fleeting joy. The destruction that follows is not their aim - it is collateral damage from a false good.

Concupiscence: Disordered Desire

This tendency toward sin is called concupiscence. It is more than sexual lust, as is often misunderstood. Concupiscence is any disordered inclination that leads us away from our ultimate good, which is God Himself.

Imagine a mechanical clock. A well-made clock keeps perfect time when properly cared for. Each part serves the whole. But if even one gear is misaligned, the entire function falters. The hands move erratically - or not at all. It cannot reliably tell you the time. Concupiscence is the internal disorder in the soul that keeps us from properly seeking our final purpose. It is not evil in itself - but it predisposes us to evil. It is a brokenness in us, a tendency toward sin.

We must confront it. In the end, we sin when we act on the disorder. Consider gluttony - we need to eat, but if we limit our portions, not eating extravagantly or excessively, we do not sin - we are not letting the disorder cause us to sin.

Even after baptism, concupiscence remains. The Catechism tells us plainly: "we must still combat the movements of concupiscence that never cease leading us into evil" (¶978).

The Church teaches that concupiscence manifests in three primary forms - already visible in the Fall of Adam and Eve, echoed in Christ's temptation, and addressed by the spiritual disciplines of the Church.

These three roots of sin - pleasure, possession, and pride - are the soil from which all other sins grow. As St. John writes: "For all that is in the world - the lust of the flesh, the lust of the eyes, and the pride of life - is not from the Father, but is from the world." - 1 John 2:16

1. Lust of the Flesh
This is the disordered craving for physical pleasure or comfort. It includes sexual sin, but also gluttony, sloth, addiction to comfort, and the rejection of sacrifice. It can manifest subtly in our pursuit of ease over virtue.
The Antidote: Fasting and chastity. The discipline of self-denial reorients the body to serve the soul.

2. Lust of the Eyes
This is the desire to possess or control what we find attractive - material wealth, power, status, even people. It drives envy, greed, and consumerism. It is not wrong to appreciate beauty or value excellence, but when we make these things our idols, we lose sight of God.
The Antidote: Almsgiving and poverty of spirit. These free us from attachment and restore trust in God's providence.

3. Pride of Life
This is the desire to be our own god - to be self-sufficient, infallible, admired, or immune to correction. It resists dependence, humility, and grace. Pride blinds us to our need for others and for God.
The Antidote: Prayer and obedience. These remind us of who we are - and who we are not - before our Creator.

We also see these in Christ's own temptation (Matthew 4; Luke 4):
- Turn stones into bread (lust of the flesh),
- Receive the kingdoms of the world (lust of the eyes),
- Leap from the temple to be glorified (pride of life).

Having no concupiscence Himself, Christ offers the antidotes: fasting, almsgiving, and prayer - the pillars of our Lenten practice and the path to freedom.

Is it not interesting, too that the vows of the religious and promises of a priest are Poverty, Chastity, and Obedience?

Why This Matters

Understanding concupiscence changes how we view evildoers.

It reminds us that many are not choosing evil outright but are deceived by a false good. Their intellect is darkened. Their will is weak. Their desire for healing or power or love is misdirected. This does not excuse sin, but does explain it. It invites a response rooted in truth and charity - not vengeance. There is a saying that hits this point: "Never attribute to malice what might be ignorance."

No one is beyond hope. Everyone can be converted, if they are willing to allow the Lord to work in their lives. And we are all, at times, the ones in need of that mercy.

This perspective equips us to hold firm to justice while still praying for the conversion of hearts. It protects us from bitterness, despair, or self-righteousness. And it prevents us from falling into the same traps we condemn in others.

The Enemy's Strategy

Satan knows our concupiscence. He exploits it. He whispers to the wounded and tempts the proud. He does not need to possess us - he only needs to deceive us.

His original lie in the Garden still echoes: "You will be like God." And too often, we believe it.

But if we learn to recognize the roots of sin, if we bring them to the light, if we allow grace to heal us - then we can break free. And then we can help others do the same.

For Reflection:
- Where do I experience concupiscence the most?
- What antidotes toward concupiscence do I need?
- How might being aware of concupiscence help give hope in the midst of evil?
- Read 1 John 2:15-17

4. What's Stopping Us from Naming Evil?

> "Sin is present in human history; any attempt to
> ignore it or to give this dark reality other names
> would be futile. To try to understand what sin is, one
> must first recognize the profound relation of man to
> God, for only in this relationship is the evil of sin
> unmasked in its true identity."
>
> – Catechism of the Catholic Church, ¶386

Rooted in Misunderstanding

Many of us fear addressing evil because we misunderstand Scripture or Church teaching. We have absorbed phrases like:
- "Do not judge, lest you be judged."
- "Love your enemies."
- "Turn the other cheek."
- "Love is patient and kind."

These are sacred truths - but they are often ripped from their context and weaponized to silence faithful Christians.

Even when we acknowledge that evil exists, we often find ourselves hesitant to name it - let alone confront it. Why?

Because naming evil *feels like* judging others. And judging others feels unloving, even un-Christian.

So, we shrink back. We bite our tongues. We blame ourselves for others' misdeeds. We tell ourselves we are being humble or charitable. In reality, we are often avoiding conflict, or worse - enabling sin.

I know this pattern well. For years, I rationalized the abusive behavior of others. I tried to excuse it, minimize it, or internalize the blame. "Maybe it was my fault." "Maybe I provoked it." "Maybe if I had only handled it better…"

But that approach only made things worse.
Unaddressed evil does not fade. It festers. It escalates. It emboldens. What we tolerate, we often perpetuate.
Worse, others may interpret our silence as permission. And when the hurt piles up - when the disrespect becomes constant and corrosive - our ability to participate in the Church's mission is compromised. Our

wounds, if left untreated, can make us wounded "wounders," to borrow from the teachings of Henri Nouwen in his book, The Wounded Healer.

Let us consider Jesus' command not to judge (Matthew 7:1). Does this mean we cannot call out sin or confront wrong? On the contrary, the Church teaches to not only speak the truth in love, but to have discernment doing so, realizing your own imperfections (i.e. humility). Jesus further elaborates by noting we should remove the log from our own eye—i.e., work out our own sin and imperfections-- so that we can help remove the speck from our brother's.

It is not about silence - it is about humble clarity!

As Pastor, I see certain struggles of my parishioners. I have to be prudent in how I approach them regarding their state – usually something to do with their marital state or something fairly public – and approach it with sensitivity, helping them to recognizing the position they are in and what remedies they may need. It takes prayer, fortitude, and wisdom, and if I go in humility, seeking truly to help, they are often open to correction because I am not condemning them, but seeking their good. I can recall times when I was not humble, and how that caused great pain to both of us. It took a long process to repair the damage an imprudent word or prideful disposition caused.

Elsewhere, St. John tells us to "test the spirits" (1 John 4:1) and to identify those motivated by lies. St. Paul exhorts us to "have nothing to do with divisive persons" (Titus 3:10) and to "expose the works of darkness" (Ephesians 5:11).

Ultimately, exposing and calling out sin cannot even be called "judgement" as the world defines it. Holiness permits and even demands discernment for the sake of truth, love, repentance, healing, and restoration. We are not to put ourselves above the sinner (for that *would* be a form of unholy judgement), but to identify with the sinner as a fellow sojourn and sinner ourselves (as St. Paul did when he named himself the "Chief of Sinners" in 1 Timothy 1:15).

Labels vs. Names
Jesus Himself used strong language - calling the Pharisees hypocrites, whitewashed tombs, even a brood of vipers. He was not name-calling out of rage, but truth-telling out of love.

There is a difference between name-calling and labeling behaviors. To say someone is acting like a wolf is not to deny their humanity - it is to accurately name the pattern of behavior so it can be addressed.

The Church has always recognized that naming sin is a Spiritual Work of Mercy. To admonish the sinner, to call out evil, to draw attention to injustice - these are not acts of aggression, but of truthful compassion.

Fear of Hypocrisy
Many hesitate to speak up because they fear being hypocritical. "Who am I to judge when I've struggled too?"

But struggling with sin does not disqualify you from helping others see theirs. A doctor recovering from the flu is still qualified to diagnose it in others. Hypocrisy is not failing to live a standard - it is pretending you are exempt from it while holding others to it.

If we speak from a place of humility and self-awareness - acknowledging our own need for grace - we are not hypocrites. We are wounded healers, which is what Christ calls all of us to be.

"Our Struggle Is Not Against Flesh and Blood..."
Some will quote Ephesians 6:12: "Our struggle is not against flesh and blood, but against powers and principalities..." True. The deeper battle is spiritual.

But that does not mean we ignore human behavior. Evil works through people, even unknowingly. To address their actions is not to deny the spiritual dimension - it is to confront its earthly consequences.

To say that "people aren't the enemy" is only helpful if we are still willing to confront the actual harm people do when they align themselves with evil, even if unintentionally.

Nice: A Four-Letter Word

Christians are often told to be "nice." But "nice" is not a Christian virtue. Kindness is. Courage is. Truthfulness is. Niceness often means silencing yourself to avoid conflict, even if it means tolerating sin or abuse.

Niceness swallows pain. Kindness confronts it - with gentleness, but also with strength.

Fear of Hurting Others

We have also confused hurt with harm. Not all pain and hurt is harmful. A surgeon uses a scalpel to cut, and that causes hurt - but to heal. Tactfully speaking a hard truth may cause momentary discomfort, but if it leads to repentance, reconciliation, or protection - it is an act of love.

On the other hand, there are those who inflict pain with no regard for healing. They manipulate, distort, control. These actions are evil, and failing to name them enables them to continue. This is harm.

Turning the Other Cheek

Many cite Jesus' teaching to "turn the other cheek" (Matthew 5:39) as a command to endure abuse without resistance. But this command has a deeper layer.

In Jesus' time, a slap was a way to degrade a social inferior. Turning the other cheek forced the aggressor to slap you with a backhand, and in doing so, confront your equal dignity. It was not an act of submission, but of silent strength - a call to repentance.

And even Jesus, who told us to love our enemies, also told the disciples to arm themselves (Luke 22:36) and overturned the tables of the moneychangers.

Christ did not tolerate evil - He confronted it, always in alignment with His mission of love.

The Blame Game

When people mistreat us, we often internalize it. "It must be me." "I'm too sensitive." "I should have done more."

But blaming ourselves for others' evil choices protects the evildoer and punishes the survivor. It perpetuates shame and prevents healing. It diminishes the image of God in us.

Yes, we all sin. Yes, we all fall short. But that truth should never be used to excuse or deflect responsibility from those who deliberately hurt others.
No amount of sin changes that. You are made in the image of God. You are worthy of dignity and truth - even if others refuse to see it.

For Reflection:
- How have I struggled with naming and addressing evil?
- What lies have I believed about evil?
- Has scripture been used against me as a way of ignoring or tolerating evil?
- Read Ephesians 5:6-20

5. How The Enemy Works

> Scripture witnesses to the disastrous influence of the
> one Jesus calls "a murderer from the beginning",
> who would even try to divert Jesus from the mission
> received from his Father. "The reason the Son of
> God appeared was to destroy the works of the
> devil." In its consequences the gravest of these
> works was the mendacious seduction that led man to
> disobey God.

> – Catechism of the Catholic Church, ¶394

Scripture is clear: evil has a source, and he is no mere metaphor.

Jesus refers to Satan as "a murderer from the beginning... a liar and the father of lies" (John 8:44). St. Peter warns us: "Be sober and vigilant. Your adversary the devil is prowling around like a roaring lion, looking for someone to devour" (1 Peter 5:8).

The devil is real. And while he is not equal to God - not all-powerful, not all-knowing, not all-present - he is cunning, persistent, and focused.

He has a strategy. And too often, we fall for it.

Satan's Primary Tactic: Deception
The devil rarely works through spectacle. He works through suggestion.

In the Garden, he did not frighten Eve. He questioned her. He seeded doubt. He offered a twisted version of the 'truth'. "Did God really say...?" "You will not die..." "You will be like God..."

The same patterns persist today. Satan deceives us by:
- Distorting God's Word.
- Sowing doubt about our identity.
- Promising false freedom.
- Exploiting our wounds and concupiscence.
- He rarely pushes; he nudges.
- He almost never shouts; he whispers.
- He loves subtlety.

Satan's Strategy: Division

One of Satan's most effective tactics is division - within ourselves, between people, and ultimately from God.

He divides:
- Mind from heart - keeping us paralyzed between what we know and what we feel.
- Person from person - through gossip, betrayal, misunderstanding, and pride.
- Soul from God - through shame, despair, or presumption.

The devil works to isolate, and once isolated, we become more susceptible to further lies and temptation.

Satan's Objective: Destruction

Jesus says plainly in John 10:10: "The thief comes only to steal, kill, and destroy."

Satan steals our peace, kills our hope, and seeks to destroy our vocation - our very selves. He targets the theological virtues:
- Faith - sowing skepticism, distraction, or indifference.
- Hope - leading us to despair, believing we are too far gone.
- Charity - hardening our hearts against God and others.

And he often does this through other people's sin - especially when we fail to name it, confront it, or heal from it.

The Devil's Tools: Accusation and Counterfeit Goods

One of Satan's most powerful roles in Scripture is "the accuser of the brethren" (Revelation 12:10).

He accuses God to us:
- "God doesn't love you."
- "He won't forgive you."
- "He's holding something back."

He accuses us to ourselves:
- "You're not good enough."
- "You're a fraud."
- "You'll never change."

And he accuses others to us:
- "They're the enemy."

- "They can't be trusted."
- "They'll never understand."

These accusations bind us in shame, resentment, and fear - often disguised as righteous conviction or pious humility.

These lies weigh us down, and we so easily believe them. I recall a number of times that I would listen to someone's story and hear the little accusations that they so easily overlooked as true. When I could gently speak a word of truth, without accusation, they would stop, and it would be as if the entire world changed because they suddenly saw the lies they had simply accepted.

Even as dangerous is the enemy's use of counterfeit goods - he mimics what is holy, twisting it enough to poison it:
- False peace that is really apathy.
- False humility that is actually self-hatred.
- False love that excuses sin or tolerates abuse.

He loves half-truths, because they are harder to detect and easier to believe.

When We Cooperate - Consciously or Not

Many people become unwitting accomplices in Satan's work - not through possession or curses, but through patterns of sin, refusal to forgive, or deliberate indifference.

This is especially painful when it happens inside the Church.

Many those involved in the church have seen or heard of it: manipulation on councils, factions in ministries or groups, gossip among staff, even spiritual abuse by those in authority. These are not "church politics" - they are spiritual battlegrounds.

Wherever truth is compromised, and wherever charity is suppressed, the devil finds a foothold.

Spiritual Warfare Is Not Only for the Dramatic

We tend to think of spiritual warfare as dramatic exorcisms or horror stories. But the real battleground is often interior - and quiet.

Spiritual warfare is also:
- Forgiving someone who does not deserve it.
- Speaking the truth when silence feels safer.
- Resisting gossip, lust, bitterness, or despair.
- Believing God's love over the enemy's accusations.

It is fought in ordinary choices - every single day.

Our Call: Be Not Afraid

Yes, the devil is real. Yes, he is dangerous. But he is also defeated.

Jesus Christ has conquered sin and death. The Resurrection was not symbolic - it was the definitive blow to the enemy's kingdom. We fight not for victory, but from victory.

Still, the battle continues until the final judgment. We are not called to ignore evil but to resist it, armed with the armor of God from Ephesians 6:
- Truth - to expose deception.
- Righteousness - to protect our hearts.
- The Gospel of Peace- that proclaims God is our peace.
- Faith - to reject fear of the Evil One.
- Salvation- which protects our intellect.
- The Word of God- which tells us the Truth.

And the Church would add:
- Charity - to disarm hatred.
- Prayer - to call on divine strength.
- Sacraments - as our armor and nourishment.

We are not sent out alone. Christ goes before us, the Spirit is within us, and the Church surrounds us.

So do not fear the battle. Fear only the silence that allows evil to grow unchecked.

For Reflection:
- How have you seen deception, division, or destruction play out in your own life?
- Where have you struggled to recognize the enemy's influence because it came through someone "good"?
- How can you better discern the enemy's tactics now?
- Read 1 Peter 56-11

6. The Tools of The Enemy

> The power of Satan is, nonetheless, not infinite. He is only a creature, powerful from the fact that he is pure spirit, but still a creature. He cannot prevent the building up of God's reign. Although Satan may act in the world out of hatred for God and his kingdom in Christ Jesus, and although his action may cause grave injuries - of a spiritual nature and, indirectly, even of a physical nature - to each man and to society, the action is permitted by divine providence which with strength and gentleness guides human and cosmic history. It is a great mystery that providence should permit diabolical activity, but "we know that in everything God works for good with those who love him."
>
> – Catechism of the Catholic Church, ¶ 395

If the devil's goal is to steal, kill, and destroy (John 10:10), then he must have weapons to do so. These weapons are not made of steel or fire. They are subtler, deadlier - aimed not at the body, but at the heart, the mind, and the soul.

Understanding these weapons allows us to recognize them in action - not only in others, but in ourselves. Once exposed, they lose some of their power. Once named, they can be resisted in the name of Christ.

Here are some of the devil's most common weapons.

1. Lies
Lies are the devil's native language. Jesus says of him: "When he lies, he speaks according to his own nature, for he is a liar and the father of lies" (John 8:44).

He lies about:
- God: "He doesn't care." "He won't forgive you." "He's punishing you."
- You: "You're worthless." "You're beyond saving." "You're the problem."
- Others: "They're against you." "They'll never change." "They don't love you."

These lies often masquerade as our own thoughts, so they sound convincing. They may echo past trauma or repeated criticism. That is part of their power.

The Counter-weapon: Truth. Scripture, the teachings of the Church, and the words of Christ are our defense. Truth cuts through lies like light pierces darkness.

2. Division
Satan thrives on division - between spouses, friends, families, communities, and especially within the Church. Where charity dies, division is born.

Division often begins subtly:
- A misunderstood comment.
- An unresolved grievance.
- A passive-aggressive action.
- A refusal to speak in truth or love.

Left unchecked, these become walls that isolate and wound.

The counter-weapon: Confession and Reconciliation. Honest communication, humility, and the willingness to forgive (and ask for forgiveness) restore unity. The Sacrament of Reconciliation is not just personal - it is communal. It is a Sacrament because it bestows grace upon grace: forgiveness for the penitent and certainty that one is reconciled with God the Father through Christ. What a glorious gift our Lord has given his beloved Church!

3. Fear
Fear can be paralyzing. The enemy uses fear to silence us, to keep us from standing up, speaking out, or moving forward.
We are fearful of so much:
- Fear of rejection.
- Fear of death.
- Fear of failure.
- Fear of being wrong.
- Fear of being found as a 'fraud.'
- Fear of being unloved.
- Fear of hell.

Often, these fears are based on half-truths: a past hurt, a real weakness, or a vulnerability. But fear is not from God. We must remember, "There is no fear in love, but perfect love casts out fear" (1 John 4:18).

The counter-weapon: Faith. Trust in God's presence, protection, and power disarms fear. When we believe that God is who He says He is, we can walk in courage - not because we are strong, but because He is.

4. Accusation
The devil is called "the accuser of the brethren" (Revelation 12:10). He accuses us constantly - reminding us of our failures, stirring up guilt without hope, replaying old wounds.

These accusations aim to paralyze us with shame. They attack our identity. They make us believe that we are what we have done - or what has been done to us.

The counter-weapon: Mercy. Confession silences the accuser. God's mercy is not reluctant - it is lavish, intentional, and always available. In Christ, there is no condemnation (Romans 8:1).

5. Isolation
Isolation is a spiritual death trap. When the enemy succeeds in convincing someone that no one understands, no one cares, or no one is safe, they become more vulnerable to his lies.

This weapon is especially effective against the wounded. Trauma, abuse, rejection, and shame can all drive someone inward, away from others - and even from God.

The counter-weapon: Community. Authentic Christian relationships are healing. The Body of Christ is not an abstract concept - it is a lived reality. In fellowship, vulnerability, and support, isolation is broken.

6. Despair
Despair is one of Satan's most prized weapons. It is the death of hope, the voice that says, "It will never change," "You'll never get better," "This is the end."

Despair leads to resignation, addiction, bitterness, even suicidal thoughts. It is a darkness that convinces us there is no light.

But despair is a lie.

The counter-weapon: Hope. Christian hope is not false optimism - it is trust in God's promises. It reminds us that resurrection follows crucifixion. That even the grave is not the end.

7. False Peace and Counterfeit Virtue

Sometimes the enemy offers "peace" that is really numbness. He counterfeits tolerance, silence, or appeasement, presenting it as maturity or kindness.

- "Let it go" becomes a way to avoid conflict.
- "Be nice" becomes a muzzle on truth.
- "Don't judge" becomes an excuse for sin.

These spiritual counterfeits are deadly precisely because they look like virtue.

The counter-weapon: Discernment. We must learn to distinguish between true peace and passive avoidance, between authentic virtue and spiritual cowardice. The Spirit gives wisdom to those who ask. That wisdom separates the right action from the wrong and helps us to do what is best for the situation.

Naming Evil Is the Beginning of Healing

The enemy's weapons are most effective when we refuse to name them. If we do not recognize the battlefield, we will always lose the fight.

Naming evil exposes it to the light of Christ which:

- Strips it of false power.
- Clarifies our response.
- Opens us to God's healing.

Evil flourishes in silence. It withers in truth.

For Reflection:

- Which of the enemy's weapons (e.g., lies, isolation, fear) has been most used against you?
- How did those weapons distort your identity or relationship with God?
- What truth do you need to replace those lies with today?
- Read Psalm 144

Part Two: The Good Shepherd Speaks
7. Jesus, The Good Shepherd: Teaching of Tender Power

> "The Church is, accordingly, a *sheepfold*, the sole and necessary gateway to which is Christ. It is also the flock of which God himself foretold that he would be the shepherd, and whose sheep, even though governed by human shepherds, are unfailingly nourished and led by Christ himself, the Good Shepherd and Prince of Shepherds, who gave his life for his sheep.
>
> – Catechism of the Catholic Church, ¶754

The Lord warned us of evildoers. He warns us that our own family members may become divided against us (Luke 12:51–53). He warns that many will hand over His followers to the powers of the world, that they will be hated because of Him. He is the Good Shepherd, and He tells that others will do evil.

In fact, in the Good Shepherd passage of John 10:1-15, he gives three specific types of evildoers - Thieves, Hirelings, and Wolves. These three images, it seems, can provide a basic framework for classifying evildoers as well as offer some insight into how to deal with their style of activity. What follows is my translation of this beautiful passage, which is an attempt to keep the original word order as much as possible.

> *1* Jesus said, "Amen, amen, I tell you, one who does not enter by the sheep fold but comes in some other way is a thief and robber. *2* But the one who enters by the entrance is the shepherd of the sheep.
> *3* For this one, the gatekeeper opens [the gate] and the sheep understand his sound/voice and he calls by name his own sheep and brings them forth. *4* When he has called out his own sheep, he goes in front of them and journeys and his sheep follow him because they know his sound. *5* But they will not follow a stranger but will run away from him they- do not understand the sound of the stranger."

6 Jesus spoke this adage to them, but they did not perceive what he was saying to them. *7* Jesus spoke once more, "Amen, amen, I tell you, I myself am (*ego eimi* - an allusion to the name of God given to Moses during the burning bush) the entrance/gate of the sheep. *8* All who came before me are thieves and robbers, but the sheep did not listen to them. *9* I myself am the entrance. Through me whoever enters will be saved and will come in and go out and will find pasture. *10* But the thief comes except to steal, and kill, and destroy fully. I myself came in order that they may have life and have it beyond measure. *11* I myself am the good (*kalos* - virtuous or morally good, able to provide the model) shepherd, the good shepherd lays down his spirit/soul/life-breath in place of the sheep. *12* The hireling/waged worker is not a shepherd, and the sheep are not his, sees the wolf coming and forsakes the sheep and vanishes, and the wolf catches the sheep and puts them to flight. *13* [The hireling flees] because he is a hireling, and he has no concern for the sheep. *14* I myself am the good shepherd, and I know mine, and mine know me, *15* According to the manner that the Father knows me and I know the Father, and I lay down my spirit in place of the sheep.

For Reflection:
- What emotions are stirred as I read this passage?
- How can I listen to the voice of the Good Shepherd?
- How do I find peace in the Good Shepherd who fiercely defends me?
- Read John 10:1-15

8. The Shepherd Who Stays and Fights

> "I am the good shepherd. A good shepherd lays
> down his life for the sheep."
>
> – John 10:11

In John 10, Jesus gives us one of the most tender and powerful images in all of Scripture: Himself as the Good Shepherd.

It is not a generic metaphor. It is deeply intentional, rooted in the Old Testament and fulfilled in Christ. And in it, we find both comfort and clarity - especially when facing evil.

A Shepherd in a World of Wolves

The context matters. Jesus does not present Himself as the Shepherd in a peaceful meadow but as an active and aggressive protector from the evil that wishes to harm those whom He loves. This is not a sentimental or idyllic pastoral scene. It is a battlefield.

The sheep are vulnerable. The threats are real. The enemies are active. And into this mess steps the Shepherd - not with a sword, but with love strong enough to lay down His life.

What Makes Him Good?

Jesus is not only a shepherd - but He is also the Good Shepherd. He is the moral exemplar of shepherds.

He contrasts Himself with the hireling who runs away at the first sign of danger. The hireling values his own safety more than the lives of the sheep. But the Good Shepherd stays. Fights. Protects. And, if necessary, dies.

He knows His sheep. Not only collectively, but intimately. Personally. He calls them by name. And they know His voice. That voice can be found only in true intimacy with the Lord.

That is not poetic fluff. It is spiritual survival.

In a world full of voices - accusations, deceptions, demands, and threats - we need to know His voice. Because that is how we know where safety lies when we are in the midst of the battle. When we come to Him, spend time with Him in prayer and holy silence, we learn His voice.

The Shepherd's Authority

The Good Shepherd does not only protect. He leads.

He goes before the sheep, guiding them to green pastures, through dark valleys, even into the sheepfold of eternity.

He does not manipulate. He does not coerce. He does not dominate.

He leads with truth and love.

And He has the authority to lay down His life - and to take it up again. His sacrifice is not a tragedy - it is a victory, a deliberate act of power and love.

The Sheep's Role

We are the sheep in this story. And while sheep are often used as a symbol of vulnerability or simplicity, in Christ's hands, they become something sacred.

To be a sheep under this Shepherd is not weakness - it is wisdom.

Sheep do not need to know the whole map. They need to know the Shepherd. They cannot fight the wolf alone. They need to stay close to the one who can.

Our role is to:
- Learn His voice through intimate prayer.
- Obey His voice.
- Follow where He leads.
- Stay within His fold.
- Trust His protection.
- Accept His healing.

Wounds and Trust

Some of us struggle to trust Christ as Shepherd because those who were supposed to protect us did not.
- Maybe a parent abandoned you.
- Maybe a spiritual leader wounded you.
- Maybe a friend betrayed you.
- Maybe you have never had a "shepherd" who protected you.

If that is you, hear this: Jesus is not like them.
He is not afraid of your wounds. He is not put off by your pain. He is not threatened by your doubts. He lays down His life - and would willingly again and again - not only in history, but in every Eucharist, every Confession, every act of mercy and grace.

Where others ran, He stays.
Where others harmed, He heals.
Where others lied, He speaks the truth.

The Good Shepherd Today
This image is not locked in the past. Christ is alive, and He is still Shepherding His people.

He does this through:
- The Sacraments - especially the Eucharist and Confession.
- Scripture - His voice made visible.
- The Church - even in her brokenness.
- Personal prayer and discernment.
- Holy friendships and community.
- Spiritual direction.

The Shepherd still speaks. Are we listening?

Why This Matters in a Book About Evil
Without this image - this truth - evil wins the narrative.

If we do not know the Good Shepherd, then the thieves, robbers, and wolves have the last word. Pain becomes permanent. Wounds define us. Bitterness replaces hope.

But if we know Him - if we trust His voice - then even in the darkest valley, we fear no evil. Because He is with us (Psalm 23:4).
We need this Shepherd now more than ever. The world is full of noise, fear, betrayal, and cruelty. But He has not left us. He walks with us. He lays down His life - for you.
And in Him, the wolves do not win.

For Reflection:
- What does it mean to you that Jesus knows you by name?
- In what areas of your life have you struggled to trust Christ as Shepherd because others failed you?
- Where is He inviting you to let Him lead again?
- Read Psalm 23

9. The Thief That Steals

> "The thief comes only to steal and kill and destroy. I
> came that they might have life and have it more
> abundantly."
>
> – John 10:10

Jesus is not vague. He draws a sharp contrast between Himself and the enemy. One gives life. The other takes it.

In this passage, Jesus is talking about false shepherds - those who come disguised as protectors but act in their own interest. He is also pointing to Satan himself, the ultimate thief.

But theft does not only happen in the spiritual realm. The thief's tactics are carried out by people - sometimes knowingly, sometimes unconsciously - who imitate the voice of the Shepherd but do not share His heart. The thief is a doer of evil.

What Does the Thief Steal?
The enemy does not come for your wallet. He comes for much more:
- Dignity - Convincing you that you are unworthy of love or respect.
- Joy - Replacing it with anxiety, guilt, or despair.
- Peace - Fostering confusion, conflict, or chaos.
- Hope - Making you believe things will never change.
- Faith - Undermining your trust in God and in others.
- Intimacy - Distorting love into control, lust, or fear.
- Identity - Defining you by your wounds instead of by God's Word.
- Purpose - Filling your time with noise so you forget why you were made.

If you have experienced deep personal hurt, you have likely felt the weight of this theft. Something precious was taken. Maybe years of your life. Maybe trust. Maybe your sense of safety. Evil always takes something that was not its to take.

While outside the scope of this book, I would like to briefly address one type of thief that is so prevalent. The porn industry preys on the vulnerable, not only the women and men who would be involved in producing it, but on those that would use it. They rob people of their dignity, offer false love, twist intimacy into lust. This industry demonstrates the thief-mentality in almost every aspect, stealing almost every area that can be stolen that we just identified. While there is debate whether there can be a true addiction to pornography, certainly we should be able to see that there is certainly compulsion – a drive to consume it that overtakes even reason itself. It enslaves and binds people.

How Does the Thief Steal?

The thief rarely breaks the door down. He often enters by deception or neglect.

- He mimics the Shepherd's voice, using spiritual language to manipulate.
- He gaslights, making you question your memory, sanity, or worth.
- He twists Scripture, making evil look holy and good look selfish.
- He feeds on silence, knowing that secrets protect sin.
- He relies on shame, ensuring you never speak up or seek help.
- He uses others, especially those in positions of trust, to do his work.

You may have encountered this kind of thief in your own story - someone who wore the mask of goodness but wounded you in private.

Some steal by intent - knowing full well what they are doing. Others steal through neglect - taking advantage of whatever situation benefits them no matter who it harms.

Both are real. Both leave scars. And neither reflects the heart of Christ.

False Voices

Jesus says His sheep know His voice. But the thief pretends to speak in His name.

These false voices sound like:

- "God doesn't want you to cause division - you must be quiet."
- "Forgiveness means pretending it didn't happen."
- "It's un-Christian to make someone uncomfortable."
- "It's prideful to think you've been wronged."
- "You're being too sensitive. You need to get over it."

These are not the voice of the Shepherd. They are the whispers of the thief. They mimic holiness but mask abuse and harm.

The Damage Done
When someone acts as a thief in your life - whether through emotional manipulation, spiritual distortion, betrayal, or abuse - the damage is real. And often, it goes unacknowledged.

Victims of spiritual or emotional theft often struggle with:
- Confusion about what is true or trustworthy.
- Self-doubt about their worth and voice.
- Guilt for even feeling hurt.
- Fear of retaliation if they speak up.
- Despair that healing is even possible.

You are not alone. The Shepherd sees. And He does not excuse the thief. He exposes him.

Christ's Response: Life Abundantly
Jesus does not only protect. He restores.

He comes to give life - not only survival, not only "coping," but abundance. Not in wealth or worldly success, but in peace, purpose, joy, and love.

Where the thief has stolen, Christ returns.
Where the thief has killed, Christ resurrects.
Where the thief has destroyed, Christ rebuilds.

But this restoration is not automatic. It begins with truth. With naming the theft. With refusing to protect the thief through silence or self-blame.

Healing comes when we:
- Invite Christ into the wound.
- Acknowledge the harm.
- Stop excusing the actions of those who steal in His name.
- Reject the lies.
- Allow others to walk with us in the healing.

You Are Worth Protecting

Maybe no one told you that before.
But you are worth protecting.
You are worth rescuing.
You are worth fighting for.
And Jesus already has.

In Him, your identity is not "the wounded," but the beloved.
Your title is not "victim," but the redeemed.
The Good Shepherd tells us through Scripture that we are:
- Children of God (John 1:12, Romans 8:16, 1 John 3:1)
- Members of the Body of Christ (1 Corinthians 12:27, Romans 12:4–5)
- Temple of the Holy Spirit (1 Corinthians 6:19–20, 1 Corinthians 3:16)
- Beloved, Chosen, & Royal Priesthood (1 Peter 2:9, Colossians 3:12)
- Citizens of Heaven & Ambassadors of Christ (Philippians 3:20, 2 Corinthians 5:20)
- Heirs with Christ (Romans 8:17, Galatians 4:7)
- A New Creation in Christ (2 Corinthians 5:17, Galatians 2:20)
- Light of the World & Salt of the Earth (Matthew 5:13–14, Ephesians 5:8)

No thief can steal your identity in Christ Jesus.
He will not let the thief have the last word.

For Reflection:
- What has been stolen from you?
- Who (or what system) in your life has acted more like a thief than a shepherd?
- What do you believe Jesus wants to restore?
- Read Psalm 62

10. The Hireling That Runs

> "The hired man, who is not a shepherd and does not
> own the sheep, sees a wolf coming and leaves the
> sheep and runs away - and the wolf snatches and
> scatters them. This is because he works for pay and
> has no concern for the sheep."
>
> – John 10:12–13

We have met the Good Shepherd - the one who lays down His life.
We have faced the thief - the one who comes to steal, kill, and destroy.
But now Jesus introduces a third character: the hireling.

The hireling is not malicious like the thief. He is not a predator. He does
not attack the sheep. He simply abandons them. He fails to do his duty.

He sees the danger and walks away.

And in that moment, his indifference becomes deadly.

The Cowardice of the Hireling

The hireling is not driven by love. He is driven by self-preservation.

He is there for the paycheck, the prestige, the image. As long as things
go smoothly, he stays. But when there's conflict, risk, or confrontation
- he runs. He protects himself, not the vulnerable.

In the eyes of the sheep, the outcome is the same as if the thief had
attacked.
The wolf snatches. The flock scatters.
The sheep are left defenseless.
And often, the hireling shrugs and says, "It's not my fight."

Modern Hirelings

Today, hirelings still exist.
They are:
- Pastors who refuse to address abuse in their parishes.
- Leaders who silence survivors to protect reputations.
- Friends who disappear when you need them most.
- Parents who stay silent while one child harms another.
- Colleagues who watch evil unfold and do nothing.

They may not intend harm. But their cowardice enables it.

When a survivor gathers the courage to speak, the hireling says:
- "That's how they are."
- "You need to forgive and move on."
- "Don't cause division."
- "Let's keep the peace."
- "God will deal with it - you only need to pray."

These phrases are not pastoral. They are self-protective. They avoid discomfort and accountability under the guise of patience or prudence.

The Pain They Cause
For those who have suffered at the hands of thieves or wolves, the abandonment of the hireling can feel even worse.

You expected the thief to steal - but not the priest to dismiss you.

You expected conflict - but not your family's silence.

You anticipated pain - but not the betrayal or abandonment of those who claimed to care.

The hireling leaves you not only wounded but also confused.
- "Was I wrong?"
- "Was it my fault?"
- "Why won't anyone stand with me?"

The hireling's refusal to act makes you question your own voice. It buries the truth under layers of self-doubt.

Why They Run
Not all hirelings are malicious. But they share one trait: they value comfort over courage.

They may be afraid of:
- Losing a position.
- Losing honor or respect.
- Starting or stirring conflict.
- Damaging relationships.
- Being seen as judgmental.
- Admitting failure.

Sometimes they have never been taught how to confront sin. Sometimes they have been survivors themselves and learned to survive through silence.

But no matter the reason, the impact is the same: vulnerability without protection.

The Tragedy of a Passive Church
When the Church behaves like a hireling, it violates its mission.

The Church is supposed to be a field hospital, not a museum. A place of protection, not passive observation. A Body that actively defends its most wounded members - not one that shields abusers to "avoid scandal."

The scandal is not only that sin exists within the Church. The greater scandal is when we refuse to confront it.

When wolves ravage, thieves steal, and hirelings run, the credibility of the Gospel is at stake.

Christ's Rebuke - and Christ's Remedy
Jesus does not mince words. He condemns the hireling's cowardice. He exposes the danger of the spiritual leaders of His day who abandon the vulnerable. And He offers Himself as the alternative.

Where the hireling runs, Christ remains.
Where the hireling deflects, Christ defends.
Where the hireling protects power, Christ protects the weak.

In Him, we find the Shepherd who never leaves.

A Word to the Wounded
If you have been hurt not only by what someone did - but by what others failed to do - please hear this:
- Your pain is real.
- Your story matters.
- Your suffering is not a burden to the Gospel - it is the very place Christ desires to heal and redeem.

You are not invisible to Him.
He does not run.

A Word to the Hireling

If you have found yourself playing the role of hireling - out of fear, ignorance, or fatigue - take courage.

It is not too late to change.

Christ does not shame you. He invites you to become a true shepherd - to stop running, to stand firm, to speak up. The sheep do not need you to be perfect. They need you to be present. To act. To protect.

Courage is not the absence of fear. It is love that refuses to let fear win.

For Reflection:
- Who left you when you needed them to stand with you?
- What did their silence teach you about your value - or about God?
- What kind of courage do you now want to offer others?
- Read Zechariah 11:4-17

11. The Wolf Among the Sheep

"The wolf snatches and scatters them."

– John 10:12

In the parable of the Good Shepherd, the wolf is the most dangerous figure.

> The thief deceives and steals.
> The hireling flees.
> But the wolf attacks.

He does not come to steal quietly or subtly. He comes with violence, to tear apart, to scatter, to devour.

The wolf is the manifestation of evil in its most brazen form. It is the wolf's nature to be evil. He is what happens when the thief's lies are believed and the hireling's silence goes unchallenged. When truth is ignored and love is distorted, the wolf moves in.

And the sheep suffer.

Who Is the Wolf?

In Scripture, wolves are a recurring image for the enemies of God's people. The wolves referred to are not the near noble pack animals we know. These wolves were solitary and often killed just for the sport of it, not for food.

Jesus warns: "Beware of false prophets, who come to you in sheep's clothing but inwardly are ravenous wolves" (Matthew 7:15).

St. Paul cautions the elders of Ephesus: "I know that after my departure savage wolves will come in among you, and they will not spare the flock" (Acts 20:29).

The wolf is not only Satan himself, but anyone who deliberately destroys others - especially the weak, the young, the trusting.

Wolves wear many faces:
- The abuser who grooms and isolates.
- The predator who hides behind charm and title.
- The manipulator who uses Scripture to silence and control.

- The narcissist who drains the soul while preserving their image.
- The unrepentant evildoer who attacks without remorse.

They are not misguided sheep. They are predators. And pretending otherwise only emboldens them.

What the Wolf Does
The wolf does not only wound. He scatters.

Victims of wolves often find themselves:
- Alienated from community.
- Disbelieved or dismissed.
- Labeled divisive or unstable.
- Isolated by shame and fear.
- Spiritually confused or despairing.

The wolf knows this. His power grows in the aftermath - not only through the harm he causes, but through the chaos he leaves behind.

How Wolves Gain Power
Wolves rarely act alone. They thrive in systems that protect them.

They gain power when:
- Hirelings look the other way.
- Communities favor image over truth.
- Victims are silenced "for the sake of unity."
- Gossip is tolerated but truth-telling is punished.
- "Forgiveness" is used as a shield for inaction.

Many wolves are skilled manipulators. They discredit their survivors before they act. They cultivate allies. They use false piety, charm, or authority as armor.

And if they are confronted, they often cry persecution. They invert the narrative so that the protector looks like the attacker, and the survivor appears unstable.

This is spiritual gaslighting - a favorite tactic of the wolf.

What the Church Must Do
The Church must not only name the wolf but act against him.

That means:
- Taking reports seriously.
- Prioritizing protection of the vulnerable and wounded over preservation of power.
- Supporting survivors without suspicion, at least listening to their stories.
- Removing predators from access to potential survivors.
- Confronting spiritual abuse with the same intensity as physical abuse.

Wolves do not repent easily. And they cannot be allowed to roam among the sheep. Mercy without accountability is not mercy. It is enablement.

What the Sheep Must Know

If you have been attacked by a wolf - emotionally, spiritually, sexually, physically - please know this:
- It was not your fault.
- You did not deserve it.
- God did not will it, though it was permitted for reasons only God knows.
- You are not what happened to you.

Wolves are real. But so is the Good Shepherd.
He saw what happened.
He did not abandon you.
And He is not finished with your story.

Christ versus the Wolf

Jesus does not negotiate with wolves. He does not downplay their behavior or ask the sheep to "be more understanding."

He drives them out.
He names them clearly.
He protects the sheep - even at the cost of His own life.

This is not soft compassion. This is holy courage.
The Shepherd does not tell you to go and make peace with the wolf. He invites you to stay close to Him, where no wolf can reach. And He promises to deal with the predator Himself.

In our day, He does this through law enforcement and the Justice system, through Church authorities, and caring adults how take justice and protection seriously. Just as He brings physical healing through the skilled doctors, surgeons, nurses, and therapists, He uses other humans to protect. But they need to be invited to help. The Church, listening to the voice of the Good Shepherd, has taken a stronger role in the protection of the flock of Christ in the wake of the sexual abuse scandals. She has taken strong steps in Her process to remove from ministry and remove from the priesthood especially those who would abuse minors. In the Appendix, I have a note addressed to those who were abused by clergy or religious. Sadly, not every Diocese or country has responded well, but continued vigilance and speaking out will bring healing so desperately needed. See also the Chapter on the Blessed Mother for some encouragement.

You Were Never Meant to Face the Wolf Alone
If this chapter resonates painfully, you are not weak. You are not crazy. You are not too broken to heal.

You are a sheep.
He is your Shepherd.
He desires to bind up your wounds and carry your home.
And the wolf does not win.

For Reflection:
- Who or what in your life has acted like a wolf?
- What helped you finally see the danger for what it was?
- What does justice - real, holy, restorative justice - look like in your story?
- Read Matthew 7:15-20

Part Three: Healing In the Pasture
12.   Holy Memory: The Beginning of Healing

> "But this I will call to mind; therefore I will hope:
> The LORD's acts of mercy are not exhausted, his
> compassion is not spent; They are renewed each
> morning - great is your faithfulness!"

Lamentations 3:21-23

We have investigated what evil is in Part One. In Part Two, we examined the Good Shepherd versus evil. Now, aware of what evil is, how it injures and wounds us, we can turn to the injuries and wounds we have received. We invite the Good Shepherd into those areas of hurt and ask for His healing, which begins by getting our mind focused in Christ.

The writer of Lamentations was no stranger to suffering. In chapter 3, his grief is so intense that he describes himself as filled with bitterness, cast into the dust, and unable to recall happiness. But then something changes. He pauses. He chooses to remember rightly: that the Lord's mercies are not exhausted but are new every morning.

That shift - from despair to hope - comes not from his circumstances changing, but from his memory being redirected to truth.

This is what the word in the New Testament for repentance, *metanoia,* really means. When we hear repentance in the Gospels, too often we think it is nothing more than turning away from sin. It is that, but so much more. It means to have a change of mind, not in the sense of a simple decision, but to see the world in a new way, to see it as God sees it. It means to put off the darkened intellect, to combat the concupiscences that tempt us, and to see the world as it truly is. It is to move from bad to good, and from good to God.

This "change of mind" is key to everything that follows in this book. Without a desire to be changed, there is no healing. And that healing begins with our memory, as the writer of Lamentations understood.

The Importance of Holy Memory

If you have suffered deeply, you may relate to the first part of this passage - the bitterness, the pain, the isolation. But you are not alone. God is at work, even when we forget. And like the prophet, we need to reclaim memory as sacred space: a place where healing begins.

The memory is a tremendous gift from God. It stores not just facts and skills, but stories, joys, sorrows, and meaning. But especially for those who have experienced trauma or abuse, memory can become distorted. This is a simple fact, not blame.

Some people suppress painful memories or blank them out. Others remember only the bad and forget the good. Still others remember everything, in high definition, with painful clarity – a gift of a great memory which can become a curse if it overwhelms. These forms of remembering can lead to hyper-vigilance, emotional flooding, or spiritual exhaustion.

No matter how your memory functions, healing often begins by allowing God to enter and restore it.

Hole-y Memory

We often do not have the full picture - even of our own lives. I am reminded of the Gospels: four evangelists, one Christ. Each records different moments, emphases, and words as they wrote their accounts of the Gospel. None contradict each other, but they give us different perspectives on the same reality. That is why the Church says, "the Gospel according to…" - each is true but shares part of the fuller Story of Jesus Christ.

Our memories are like that. We might have a limited view of an event until someone else shares their experience or until years later we gain greater insight. Healing happens as the gaps begin to be filled and the missing pieces restored.

Wholly Memory

Sometimes, though, we remember everything - and it is too much. When we remember too much, all the data can be overwhelming. We need to be able to sort through all of it to find the heart of the matter. We need to process it. And for that, we need help.

For all of us, sometimes that means talking to someone else who was there, or a trusted spiritual director, or simply someone who could help us see with new eyes. Processing our memories - gently, honestly, and prayerfully - can bring clarity and freedom. They help us tell the story.

Only then can we bring those memories into the light of Christ. Not to erase them, but to purify them. And in purifying them, we begin to heal by remembering rightly.

This purification is part of our journey toward holiness. In spiritual tradition, the path to holiness has three steps: purification, illumination, and union. We will encounter this pattern throughout the book. We purge, bring to the light, and grow closer to Christ. We remember, though, that it is Christ who draws us into union with Him, it is not a work on our own.

A Process for Healing Memories

This kind of healing is a form of prayer. I am not a psychologist, and this book is not a substitute for professional care. But spiritually, here is a model that helped me - first with guidance, and then on my own in prayer:

1. **Ask for the Holy Spirit to guide you.**
   Invite the Spirit to guide, protect, and bring forth only what is ready to be healed.
2. **Let the memory surface.**
   Pay attention to what emotions arise. Do not judge them - just notice.
3. **Invite Jesus into the memory.**
   Ask Him to show where He was, what He wants you to know, or how He wants to act.
4. **Ask your questions.**
   "Why did You allow this?" "Where were You?" "What do You want me to do with this pain?"
5. **Listen. Be still and know He is God.**
   Often, healing comes not with fireworks, but with peace. Be patient. Be in holy silence.
6. **Let Him heal.**
   Allow Him to protect what was vulnerable, heal what was wounded, and speak truth into lies.
7. **Check back on those emotions.**

Was there any change? A softening, a clarity, or a sense of what action you need to take to move forward.

8. **Ask for your response.**

It may be forgiveness. It may be grieving. It may be letting go. It may be simply resting in His presence.

Some memories need to be released. Others need to be reframed. Still others need to be seen with Christ beside you to be redeemed.

You are not meant to carry painful memories alone. Healing memory is part of healing the whole self. When our memory becomes whole, we are made more holy.

Reflection Questions
- Are there memories I avoid because they are too painful or confusing?
- How have I seen God begin to bring clarity or healing to a memory I once feared?
- What would it look like to invite Jesus into one memory this week - to sit with it, not alone, but with Him?
- Read Lamentation 3

13.   You're Allowed to Be Angry

"Be angry, but do not sin."

– Ephesians 4:26

For many Christians, anger feels like a failure.

We are taught that love is patient.
That kindness is a fruit of the Spirit.
That Jesus forgave from the Cross.
That real holiness is calm, gentle, and sweet.

So when we feel angry - especially in the wake of abuse, betrayal, or injustice - we often assume something is wrong with us.

But Scripture says otherwise.

The Psalms are full of angry, messy prayers. Some call out for sinful vengeance against one's enemies (Psalm 137:9 especially, and while a human reality, such feelings need to be addressed, not acted on in sinful ways). While such verses are disturbing, we remember that they are not models of how to behave, but rather showing us to pray into the pain, vengeance, or hard feelings to allow the Lord to heal.

In the Garden of Gethsemane, during our Lord's Agony in the Garden, He prayed so intensely that He sweat blood. While not anger, He shows He is accustomed to our messy prayers and emotions. The Letter to the Hebrews teaches that He is accustomed to our weakness though sinless (Hebrews 4:15) and offered loud cries and supplication and was heard (Hebrews 5:7) In the Garden, He united His will to the will of the Father to accept the chalice of suffering He was to partake on the Cross. It was filled with honest, raw, and heart-wrenching prayer.

And there is His cry from the Cross. This is more than our Lord referring to the beginning of the Psalm 22 as a reference to the hope found at the psalm's conclusion. It was also about feeling abandoned by the Father. As He was crucified, He felt the full weight of every sin, every choice against God, ever act of abuse and neglect. How could he feel anything but abandonment?

You are allowed to be angry, but let it be without sin, possible in Christ.

Anger Is a Human Emotion - Not a Sin
Anger is not evil in itself. It is not a character flaw.

It is an emotional response to something being wrong or unjust. Some people might be more attuned to what is wrong.

Anger says:
- "This should not have happened."
- "This crossed a line."
- "This violated what is good and right."

Anger is part of your God-given emotional system.

It is not a sin, it is a sign.

Even God Gets Angry
Throughout Scripture, God is described as:
- Slow to anger (Psalm 103:8).
- Righteous in His anger (Deuteronomy 32:35).
- Provoked to anger by injustice and idolatry.

Jesus - God Incarnate - felt anger.
- He called out spiritual leaders who abused their power with fierce clarity.
- He burned with holy fire when people distorted His Father's house enough to turn over tables

If Christ can be angry without sin, so can you, with His grace.

Righteous Anger vs. Destructive Rage
There is a difference between:
- Anger that leads to truth,
- Anger that leads to harm.

Righteous anger:
- Names injustice.
- Honors boundaries.
- Protects the vulnerable.
- Moves toward truth, justice, and restoration.

Unrighteous anger:
- Seeks revenge.
- Controls others.
- Lashes out.
- Refuses forgiveness.
- Becomes wrath - unbalanced, vindictive, unjust.
- Causes harm and destruction.

Anger becomes dangerous and sinful not because we feel it - but because we refuse to direct it rightly.

Suppressed Anger Becomes Poison
When anger is denied, it does not disappear.
It goes underground - and comes out as:
- Depression.
- Anxiety.
- Resentment.
- Emotional numbness.
- Passive-aggressive behavior.
- Self-hatred.

You cannot heal what you are not allowed to feel.
God does not ask you to pretend. He asks you to be honest - and bring it to Him.

What Anger Is Trying to Tell You
Anger reveals your values.

It shows you what you love - and what you fear losing.
- If you are angry that someone betrayed your trust, it means you value loyalty.
- If you are angry about manipulation, it means you care about truth.
- If you are angry at injustice, it means your heart is alive and desires justice.

Your anger may be the clearest sign that you are still healthy enough to care. Apathy shows that nothing matters, and that is a form of sloth.

What to Do with Your Anger

1. Name it!
2. Say what you are feeling. Without apology.
3. Bring it to God. He can handle it.
4. Do not bury it - or detonate it. Acknowledge it what is hurting
5. Let it speak. Let it move you. But do not let it control you.
6. Channel it into the right action. Into truth-telling. Into protection. Into justice. Into boundaries. Into prayer.

Righteous anger can become holy action.

Holy Anger Is Not Bitterness

Bitterness is anger that refuses to release control.
Bitterness says, "By your actions, you took something from me, and I won't be okay until I get it back from you."
Bitterness says, "I will never be okay until you fix it."

Anger says, "That was wrong."

God does not condemn your anger.
He invites you to bring it to Him - so it can be transformed, not suppressed.

You Don't Need to Be Ashamed of Your Fire

Some people will tell you:
- "Let it go."
- "That's not loving."
- "Don't be so dramatic."
- "Real Christians don't get this upset."

But your fire of anger is not the problem.
What happened to you is.

Do not confuse holiness with passivity.
Do not confuse anger with sin.

Let Anger Lead You to Truth

Let it name the wrong.
Let it protect what matters.
Let it fuel your healing.
Let it remind you that something holy still burns in you.
And when the time is right, let it go - not because it was wrong to feel it, but because you are not meant to carry it forever.

God is the Final Judge, who makes all things right in His time. Justice will be carried out, either on earth or on the final day of judgement. Let the Good Shepherd, the Prince of Peace, guide you through your anger and let Him have the final say when the day of justice comes.

For Reflection:
- What are you angry about - and what have you done with that anger?
- Where have you felt ashamed of your righteous fire?
- How can you begin to let anger lead you toward healing instead of hiding?
- Read Luke 22:39-46

14. Great Expectations: Dealing With Resentment

> "Now the people were filled with expectation..."
>
> – Luke 3:15

At first glance, this verse may seem out of place in a book about forgiveness and healing. But it speaks deeply to the human experience of waiting, longing - and often, of being disappointed.

As John the Baptist offered a baptism of repentance, the people wondered if he might be the long-awaited Messiah. Their hearts were filled with expectation. But imagine their disappointment when they realized this strange man - clothed in camel's hair, eating locusts and wild honey - was not The One. And if he had not pointed them toward Jesus, their unmet expectations might have turned into frustration, even resentment, wrath.

That is the danger of expectation.

It is not unlike what happened at Jesus' trial. The religious leaders demanded a clear answer from Him: "Are you the Messiah?" (Luke 22:67). But they did not get the kind of Messiah they expected - and their disappointment turned to rage.

Unmet Expectations and the Roots of Resentment

Unmet expectations are a major source of anger, hostility, and broken trust. But not all expectations are created equal.

Realistic Expectations:

These are reasonable, human expectations - like the expectation to be treated with dignity, or not to be harmed. When these are violated, anger can be righteous and healing, especially when acknowledged and addressed in holy and appropriate ways.

Unrealistic Expectations:

These are impossible or unfair. For example, expecting a child to meet your emotional needs, or a flawed parent to love perfectly, is impossible. Holding someone to a standard they cannot possibly meet - especially without communicating it - can poison a relationship.

Spoken vs. Unspoken Expectations:
Even realistic expectations can cause hurt if they are never communicated. Unspoken expectations leave the other person unaware of what is needed - yet they are often punished for failing to deliver.

But the most damaging of all are unspoken, unrealistic expectations. These lead to chronic disappointment and deep resentment. We begin to judge others not only for failing, but for failing in ways they could not have known or prevented.

A Theological Lens
This is not only relational psychology - it is a spiritual truth.

In moral theology, we recognize that some laws must be revealed (like the call to worship God on the Sabbath), while others can be known through natural law (like the command not to kill). The human heart bears a moral imprint. In the same way, we should consider: Is this expectation something the other could have known, should have known, or could reasonably fulfill?

If not, holding on to resentment is unjust - and unhealed resentment becomes a spiritual wound.

What Resentment Reveals
Resentment often signals more than only anger. It points to a deeper story:
- A longing that went unmet.
- A wound that was never seen.
- A false hope that quietly shaped your view of someone.

Unhealed resentment does not only strain relationships - but it also stains them. It leaks into tone, body language, assumptions, and even prayer. It can build walls that shut out the very healing we seek.

That is why resentment must be named, examined, and surrendered.

A Prayer for Letting Go of Resentment
This prayer is not about assigning blame or demanding an apology. It is about honestly acknowledging what you are holding and placing it into Jesus' hands. These are not a simple one-time prayer – they often need to be repeated, not because they did not help, but that the wound, the

pain, the anger is so much deeper, and the Lord desires to heal to the root.

1. Start by naming the resentment and who it is directed toward. Then pray:
   > "Holy Spirit, shine the light of your love into my heart. Reveal to me the emotions of resentment that I may be harboring - toward You, others, or myself."

2. Wait quietly as each emotion surfaces.
   > "Jesus, I relinquish control of this resentment toward (name). Please take it away."

3. Then pause, pray in silence. Notice if it has left. Continue as needed.

4. If sinful judgment or condemnation remains, you may pray:
   > "Jesus, today I choose to forgive (name). Please take this judgment away."

5. Once the resentment is removed, ask the Holy Spirit to reveal the deeper wound beneath it. Healing the root will keep the wall from returning.

Reflection Questions
- What expectations have I carried - spoken or unspoken - that may have been unrealistic or unfair?
- Is there someone I resent for failing to meet my needs or hopes? What might I need to release them from?
- What wound or longing might be hidden beneath my resentment - and how might I invite the Lord to heal it?
- Read Ephesians 4:25-32

15.   The "If" Game: Regret

> "For godly sorrow produces a salutary repentance
> without regret, but worldly sorrow produces death.
>
> – 2 Corinthians 7:10

Many people who experience evil, abuse, or trauma fall into playing a familiar, painful game. It is called the "if" game - and it sounds like this:
- If I were stronger, wiser, older...
- If only I had seen the warnings...
- I wish I had only spoken up sooner...

The implication behind each of these thoughts is the same: If I had done something different, maybe the pain could have been avoided.

A related version of this is the "Woulda, Coulda, Shoulda" game. We replay scenes in our minds, imagining how we could have acted differently - what we should have said, how we could have left sooner, how everything might have changed. Sometimes we do this to make sense of the pain. But often, it is a subtle form of self-blame, a way of claiming control over something that was never ours to carry.

At the root of these games is regret - the grief of what might have been.

But not all regret is the same.

Worldly Regret: Shame and Scrupulosity
What might initially appear as regret is sometimes shame or scrupulosity. These try to negate Christ's grace and forgiveness, and whisper that you are beyond God's help and redemption. It leads to hopelessness, despair, and spiritual exhaustion.

Shame and Scrupulosity are the destroyers of faith. They are not grounded in truth, but rather in a belief that:
- God hates you,
- You are a bad person.
- You are unworthy of grace.

Scrupulosity is closely related to Obsessive-Compulsive Disorder (OCD), specifically the compulsive repetition of certain actions, prayers, or formulas in an attempt to control one's internal anxiety or external circumstances. Both scrupulosity and OCD involve obsessive fear of doing something wrong, often including a deep anxiety about offending God, excessive confession or self-examination, difficulty accepting forgiveness, and an overwhelming sense of responsibility.

OCD is a recognized psychological disorder that may involve any kind of obsession—moral, relational, physical, or otherwise—with or without a religious component. It often distorts one's self-identity and impairs daily functioning. OCD typically requires treatment from a trained psychologist, though the religious expressions of it can sometimes be addressed alongside therapy by a wise and competent spiritual director.

Scrupulosity, while it may overlap with OCD, is primarily spiritual in nature. It is a distortion of God's mercy, replacing trust in His love with fear of His punishment. The scrupulous soul doubts God's forgiveness and lives with an overbearing sense of sinfulness, sometimes believing that even morally neutral or innocent actions could lead to damnation. Religious practice becomes fear-driven rather than love-led.

In the confessional, scrupulosity often shows up as:
- Repeated confessions of the same sinful actions or thoughts.
- Over-analysis of one's words or actions.
- Use of multiple synonyms for a single fault.
- A paralyzing fear that the "right" formula hasn't been used.
This can lead to despair.

A gentle, consistent confessor and/or experienced spiritual director can be an anchor for someone struggling with this painful burden. The healing journey requires replacing fear with trust, and remembering that God desires mercy, not torment. His grace is bigger than our feelings, and His love is not earned but given.

St. Alphonsus Ligouri has a brochure on scruples simply titled "Instructions for the Scrupulous" or in other translations, "Instructions for Those Who Have Scruples." It is difficult to find, but in this brief brochure he advises:
- Do not repeat confessions or doubts unless there is absolute certainty that something was not properly confessed.
- Do not delay reception of Holy Communion out of fear of being unworthy unless truly aware of mortal sin (see Chapter 1 for more on Mortal Sin).

- Trust the confessor's judgment over your own feelings.
- Refrain from re-examining past confessions, as it leads to torment, not holiness.
- Scruples are not sins but temptations—and should be treated as such.
- Peace and obedience are signs of progress, while constant anxiety demonstrates more healing is needed.

Historically, scrupulosity has often found expression in certain cultural and theological movements marked by spiritual rigorism. One such movement was Jansenism, which gained influence in 17th-century France. Jansenists emphasized human unworthiness, rejected the accessibility of God's grace, and discouraged frequent reception of the Eucharist, teaching that only a small number were truly worthy of Communion.

In response, St. Alphonsus Liguori passionately defended the mercy of God and encouraged frequent, trust-filled reception of the sacraments—especially for the scrupulous. Around the same time, the Lord revealed His Sacred Heart to St. Margaret Mary Alacoque, showing His heart wounded and burning with love for humanity.

This devotion to the Sacred Heart, with its focus on Christ's tender and merciful love, remains a powerful antidote to scrupulosity. For those who struggle with spiritual fear, the Sacred Heart reminds us: God desires not perfection, but trust. Not fear, but relationship.

Shame, on the other hand, burdens us with the illusion that we could have prevented the evil done to us, if only we had been smarter, faster, braver, stronger. It does not allow us to allow God to forgive us for sins we have committed or heal us of wounds we endured. Even when we later repented of our part of what was sinful, the shame comes back to destroy the grace provided to us in reconciliation. It mires us in sinful regret where we live in the past, instead of looking forward to the future in God's grace, as a redeemed Child of God!

Shame from an unholy regret often afflicts survivors of abuse or trauma, especially those who were young when it happened. For example, some victims tell themselves, "If I had been older or stronger, I could have stopped the abuse." People who have not experienced trauma know this is not true. But shame blocks the ability for the victim to discern truth:

that it was not the victim's fault, that they had no power or knowledge to stop the abuse, and that the abuser, not the victim, is at fault. Grace and truth are the solution to shame and these starts at the cross of Christ and a proper perspective on what Godly sorrow is.

Godly Regret: Sorrow That Heals

Some regret can lead to clarity and healing. This kind of sorrow does not deny the pain or minimize the wound. It simply names what should not have happened - and affirms that it did. And this is a form of grief.

It may even bring us to a deeper realization as we say to ourselves: "I did not have the strength back then. I did not know what to do. But I did survive. I am here. And by God's grace, I am growing."

This kind of regret leads to mercy. First, we accept mercy toward ourselves - for not being perfect, for not knowing what we could not have known. Then, perhaps, we might offer mercy toward the one who failed us - not excusing them but naming the truth without vengeance.

This is mercy with teeth: it holds people accountable in love, refusing to rewrite the past or enable the lie. But it also opens the door for redemption - on our side and theirs.

God Redeems Regret

God can redeem even our regrets.

He purifies them in the light of truth and love. He forgives our sins when we confess them. He can bring good out of what hurt us - even when we cannot see how. Even our regrets, if surrendered, are already factored into the great story of salvation He is writing through our lives.

If we hand Him our theoretical "what-ifs,"
He will show us His realistic "what is."

And sometimes - miraculously - we may even come to thank Him, not for the wound, but for the wisdom, the mercy, the courage we never would have found otherwise.

Reflection Questions:
- What regrets have I been carrying that may not be rooted in truth?
- Can I name one area of my life where God has already redeemed something I once grieved? Do I keep bringing up this redeemed area and what is a proper Christian response to this?
- How might I offer my regret to Christ - not to erase the past, but to invite Him into it?
- Read Psalm 32

16. Guilt Versus Shame

> Deep within his conscience man discovers a law
> which he has not laid upon himself but which he
> must obey. Its voice, ever calling him to love and to
> do what is good and to avoid evil, sounds in his heart
> at the right moment... For man has in his heart a law
> inscribed by God... His conscience is man's most
> secret core and his sanctuary. There he is alone with
> God whose voice echoes in his depths.
>
> – Catechism of the Catholic Church, ¶ 1776, Vatican
> II Gaudium et Spes 16

Catholics are often teased for what some call "Catholic guilt." But if you scratch the surface, what many people experience is not guilt - it is shame. And those two are vastly different.

Guilt is the recognition that we have done something wrong - that we failed to do the good or chose to do the bad. It is the conscience stirring within us. Conscience is the voice God placed in our hearts, calling us to return to what is right. Guilt leads to remorse- an acknowledgement that I did wrong that moves me to repentance.

Shame, like we touched on in the previous chapter, attacks the person rather than the behavior. Shame says:
- I am wrong.
- I am bad.
- I am stupid.
- I am unworthy.

It is the voice of brokenness, often magnified by abuse or trauma, that tries to convince us we are our sins - or worse, the sins committed against us.

Guilt is a movement of grace - a prompting toward confession and healing. It is a gift from God.

Shame shuts us down. It silences us. It convinces us that we are too far gone to be loved. It is often a tool of the Evil One or the result of our own brokenness.

There is no mercy in shame - unless it is brought into the light of Christ where shame can be called out and be brought to heal by Truth. Guilt, though painful, can be a form of mercy with teeth. It stings - but it heals. It tells the truth, but it leads us home.

Sadly, evil often weaponizes shame. What begins as guilt over a mistake or a sin can become a tool of manipulation. We begin to believe not only that we have done wrong - but that we are wrong, unforgivable, evil.

That is why naming the truth matters. When we learn to discern between guilt and shame, we begin to reclaim our voice. With the Lord's help, we can reclaim our story.

Reflection Questions
- When I feel burdened by something I have done (or failed to do), can I tell whether it is guilt or shame I am feeling?
- Have I ever experienced shame because of someone else's sin or manipulation? How did it affect the way I saw myself or God?
- What steps can I take to bring shame into the light - through prayer, confession, or trusted support - so it can be transformed by mercy?
- Read Romans 8:1-13

17. Saying "I'm Sorry" Is Not Enough: Remorse

> The confession (or disclosure) of sins, even from a
> simply human point of view, frees us and facilitates
> our reconciliation with others. Through such an
> admission man looks squarely at the sins he is guilty
> of, takes responsibility for them, and thereby opens
> himself again to God and to the communion of the
> Church in order to make a new future possible.

> Catechism of the Catholic Church, ¶ 1455

Confession of sins leads to reconciliation. The Catechism affirms this reality not only in the Sacrament of Reconciliation, but also in the way human beings relate to one another. When we acknowledge wrongdoing, truly and humbly, there is hope.

But not every apology leads to reconciliation. This is simply because not every apology is a confession.

The Problem with "I'm Sorry"

Many of us were taught as children to say, "I'm sorry" - even when we did not mean it. Those forced apologies, usually muttered under our breath, often sounded more like "Let me say this so I can get out of trouble" rather than a sincere act of contrition.

Unfortunately, many adults do not get much better.

Two Common Extremes

Over-apologizing

Many wounded people - especially survivors of abuse - develop a habit of apologizing for everything.
- "I'm sorry I'm in the way."
- "I'm sorry I have needs."
- "I'm sorry for being upset."

In extreme cases, we even apologize for the sins of others. This comes not from guilt, but from internalized shame or an unhealthy co-dependency.

Never apologizing
Others - especially those hardened by pride or hurt - may go to the other extreme.
- They avoid responsibility.
- They minimize harm.
- They rarely, if ever, say the words, "I was wrong."

For some, especially those with deep narcissism or personality disorders, true empathy is blocked, making authentic contrition nearly impossible.

The Anatomy of a Bad Apology
We have all heard these:
- "I'm sorry you feel that way."
- "I'm sorry... but you misunderstood me."
- "I'm sorry, but you made me do it."
- "I'm sorry *(I got caught)*."

These are not apologies. They shift blame, offer no admission of guilt, and make reconciliation impossible.

Slightly better attempts are:
- "I'm sorry, I didn't mean to..."
- "I'm sorry, I'll do better..."

These can ring hollow if there is no accountability or concrete change.

What Makes an Apology Real?
A genuine apology has several key marks:
- Admission of guilt - no excuses, no blame-shifting.
- Acknowledgment of the hurts caused.
- Sincerity - spoken with humility and remorse.
- A plan for change - specific and realistic.
- No pressure for immediate forgiveness.
- Respect for the wounded person's pace.

Example:
"I'm sorry I spoke behind your back. It was wrong, and I know it hurt you. I'll work to be more honest and respectful moving forward. I hope you can forgive me when you're ready."

This kind of apology allows healing to begin.

Consider the near perfect apology of the so-called Prodigal Son of Luke 15. This young son asks his father for his inheritance, an act akin to asking the father to die. The father lovingly does so, dividing his estate between his sons, leaving nothing for himself. The younger son takes it, squanders it, and has nothing left. When famine hits, and he is left wanting to eat the slop of the pigs, which as a Jew he should not have been touching. He realizes his sin and error. He composes an apology and begins the journey home. His father runs to him, embraces him, and forgives him, but the son is able to say part of it:

> 'Father, I have sinned against heaven and against
> you; I no longer deserve to be called your son.'

It is an admission of guilt and wrongdoing, remorse, and leaves the decision in his father's hands. His practiced apology, no less sincere, displays that he is prepared to be treated as a farm hand! I say so called because it is the father who is lavish, the meaning of 'prodigal,' lavish in wealth, forgiveness, and love.

Why "I'm Sorry" Isn't Always Enough

When the wound is deep, a quick "I'm sorry" can feel like a band-aid over a bullet wound. Or worse, like a dismissal of the pain altogether.

It does not only fail to heal - but it can also reopen the wound.

Remorse is the recognition that there was a wrong done or a good that was left undone. It carries a true sorrow for the pain those actions or inactions caused. Remorse is a key part for true reconciliation.

Some people lack the capacity for true remorse. They may say sorry only to manipulate, avoid consequences, or keep control.
- You can still forgive someone who is not sorry - but that forgiveness is for your sake, not theirs.
- You can forgive someone who shows no remorse - but trust may not be restored.
- You can forgive someone who denies wrongdoing - but reconciliation may not be possible.

Forgiveness is your call.
Reconciliation is their responsibility too.
And "I'm sorry" is only the beginning.

For Reflection:
- Have I ever heard a good apology, either to me or someone else, that made me feel seen, heard, respected?
- How can I move on from the lack of a genuine apology?
- Read Luke 15:11-32

18. Holy Honesty: Dealing with Hard Emotions

A clean heart create for me, God; renew within me a
steadfast spirit.

– Psalm 51:12

One of the most important things we need to learn on the road to healing is this: Our emotions are not sinful in themselves. They are feelings, a response that affects our mood. But when we act on those feelings, we can either act in holiness or in sin.

These feelings are 'loud' - they cannot be suppressed or ignored forever. They must be listened to.

If you are reading this book, you have likely been hurt. And when we have been hurt - especially by someone who was supposed to love or protect us - our emotional world can feel like a minefield: full of anger, sorrow, regret, even hatred. These feelings are not polite or neat. Most of us have been taught, especially in religious environments, to silence them.

Worse, those who have been abused are often told - implicitly or explicitly - that certain emotions should not be expressed. It might have been through unmet emotional needs, being told something like "suck it up" or "man up," or, in the spirit of that familiar Disney lyric, to "conceal, don't feel." We learn the need to repress what is most intense. At some point, those emotions may begin to suffocate us spiritually. In the most severe moments, they can feel like they are taking our breath away. And so, we suppress those emotions. In fact, sometimes we suppress them so much that we become unable to identify them accurately, at least at first. I have included a table in the Appendix that may help.

Big emotions do not go away because we ignore them. They come out sideways, in depression, anxiety, avoidance, or destructive behavior. They begin to heal only when they are brought into the light - honestly, gently, and with Christ.

A Personal Memory
When I was in sixth grade, a friend from another school invited me to a sleepover. The next day, due to a school conflict, everyone had to bring

lunch from home. My brother did not bring my lunch *on purpose*, so I had to miss eating lunch for that day.

I was not upset about the possibility of going hungry - I knew I would not starve. I was hurting, so now I sat in the back of the classroom, silent tears sliding down my face.

I did not yet have the vocabulary for what I was feeling. I only knew I was sad - and ashamed that anyone could see it.

It was my teacher - a wise, grandmotherly woman - who gently told the class, "Sometimes people just feel sad and need to cry." That simple sentence by my teacher gave me something I had not known I needed: permission to feel without shame.

Then something remarkable happened. My classmates noticed, and instead of teasing me, they quietly offered their help: a quarter of a sandwich, some carrots. They thought it was about the meal, I knew that it was something more that I hungered—love and acceptance. Only later did I understand what it was. God gave me grace later to see that my classmates' response was His means of helping me through this difficult time.

That story still matters.
Not because it was dramatic.
But because it was the first time that I remember someone named my emotions as valid and gave me space to feel them.

So now, I offer you the same permission: to name and feel your own.

Naming Emotions Before God
We have already explored some of the hard emotions - anger, regret, resentment. Now we turn to the holy work of naming them - with truth, and with God.

Sometimes, people rush to say, "God, I forgive them," or "God, I'm not angry," because they think that is what they are supposed to say. But the Lord prefers honest prayers - even angry ones - over polished lies.
He already knows what you are feeling. And He wants you to live in the truth.
  -   If you are angry, tell Him.

82

- If you are grieving, say so.
- If you do not know how to forgive, start there.

That is the kind of honesty He can work with.
That is the kind of prayer He always answers with His peace and understanding.

A Simple Process for Difficult Emotions: AHHH - Acknowledge, Hand Over, Hear, Heal

When emotions feel overwhelming, this simple process can help you bring them to Christ with honesty and hope. It may even help you breathe again:

1. **Acknowledge** what you are feeling.
   When the emotions rise to the surface, we need to allow them. Let them flow - so they can begin to go. Do not judge them. Name them honestly. This may be delayed briefly, perhaps, if you are not in a place to fully process, but when you are, bring them to the Lord.

2. **Hand them over** to the Lord.
   Say aloud or silently: "Jesus, I give You this [anger, fear, grief, bitterness, regret, resentment, remorse]. Take it. Purify it in Your truth."

3. **Hear** what He says in return. This means being quiet, waiting for Him.
   Be still. Listen for a word of comfort, challenge, or insight. It may come through a Scripture passage, a memory, or a deep sense of peace.

4. **Heal** with the grace He offers.
   Receive what He is giving - love, mercy, strength, clarity. And take a small step forward in that grace.

Acknowledge. Hand over. Hear. Heal.

We must admit our hard emotions. We may need to take a breath, to breathe in and out, as we name what we are feeling, and as we share with the Lord,
and listen to Him,
we could move on,
just by watching our breath.
In and AHHH...

And He is faithful, if we truly take that moment and honestly acknowledge it and accept the gift He offers.

That is how the Lord leads us into healing.
Let Him carry what is too heavy.
Let Him sort what is holy and what is harmful.
He is gentle enough to handle it all.
And He will give strength to move on.

Final Word
There is no healing without honesty.
No mercy without truth.
No resurrection without going through the tomb.

These emotions are not your enemy.
They are invitations - sometimes loud and painful - to return to the One who already knows how you feel. Learn to breathe again. Allow yourself to feel them.

Bring them to Him.
Even your ugliest emotions are not too much for Christ. He has felt them with you.

Reflection Questions
- What emotions have I been afraid to admit to God or others?
- Have I ever mistaken emotion for sin? What needs to be confessed - and what needs to be comforted?
- What would it look like to invite Christ into one painful emotion today?
- Read Psalm 139

19. The Power of Naming

> "God brought them to the man to see what he would
> call them, and whatever the man called each living
> creature, that was its name."

> – Genesis 2:19

There is power in naming. In Scripture, naming is one of the first acts of authority that God gives to humanity.

In the Garden of Eden, Adam was entrusted with naming the animals - not only as a task, but as a sign of loving dominion, understanding, and relationship.

To name something is to:
- Bring it into the light.
- Define its nature or essence.
- Distinguish it from everything else.
- Take away its power to hide.
- Know what harm or good it can cause.
- Begin to understand it.

And the same is true when we name the wounds we carry.

Evil Thrives in the Unnamed

Many survivors of abuse, betrayal, or mistreatment struggle to describe what happened to them. They say things like:
- "It wasn't that bad."
- "I don't want to exaggerate."
- "Maybe it was only a misunderstanding."
- "He was only really stressed."
- "I think I'm overreacting."
- "She didn't mean to hurt me."

Why? Because evil wants to remain vague. It wants to be hidden.

The enemy whispers, "It's fine. You're fine. Don't say it aloud."

But when we name evil for what it is - abuse, control, gaslighting, betrayal, manipulation - we strip it of its ability to confuse us.

Naming is clarity. Naming is strength. Naming is the beginning of freedom.

Jesus Names Evil
Jesus did not avoid naming sin.
He called out hypocrisy.
He named greed (Luke 12:15, Mark 7:21-22, Matthew 23:25).
He told Peter, "Get behind me, Satan," when Peter resisted the Cross.
He addressed the devil directly in the wilderness - and later, in others.
He did not only "feel uncomfortable" and remain silent when He witnessed the desecration of the Temple - He flipped tables and declared, "You've turned My Father's house into a den of thieves."

Naming is not anger out of control.

Naming is truth in service of justice.

What Naming Does for the Wounded
When you name what happened to you, you:
- Stop protecting the person who hurt you.
- Begin to believe yourself.
- Stop carrying someone else's guilt and shame.
- Invite others into your world.
- Find your God-given strength.
- Make space for the Holy Spirit to heal and reorder what has been broken.

You cannot forgive what you cannot name.

You cannot repent of sin you will not identify.

And you cannot heal from a wound you are not allowed to describe.

Naming Doesn't Mean Cursing
There is a difference between naming something honestly and speaking in hatred.

Naming says:
- "That was emotional abuse."
- "That was spiritual manipulation."
- "That was neglect."

86

- "That was gaslighting."
- "That was sinful."

It is not bitterness. It is truth.
It does not curse. It does not condemn.
But it also does not cover up. It does not excuse. It does not sanitize what God calls evil.

What If I Don't Know What to Call It?
That is okay, for a time.
Sometimes all we can say is:
- "Something was wrong."
- "That hurt more than I expected."
- "I still think about it, and it makes me tremble."
- "I don't know what to call it, but I know it wasn't love."

You do not have to have the perfect word. But you do have permission to start speaking. And with time, the language will come.

Naming Doesn't Always Lead to Resolution
Naming the truth does not guarantee that others will agree, apologize, or change.
- Sometimes, they will deny it.
- Sometimes, they will accuse you of being dramatic.
- Sometimes, they will leave.

But your naming is not for them - it is for you.
It is a response to God's grace and to live in the truth.
It is for your freedom.

God Loves When You Tell the Truth
Even when you are the only voice.
Even when you are a little scared.
Even when no one else believes you.
Even when naming means someone is walking away.
Even when it changes everything.
Keep telling the truth.
God loves the truth.
God is the truth.
And He rejoices when His children proclaim it.

Name It - And Let It Go

When you name what happened, you are not holding onto it forever.
You are bringing it into the light so that it can be transformed.
It is no longer your secret burden.
It is no longer your shame.
It becomes part of your story - but not the end of it.
The power of evil is broken the moment we call it what it is and place it in Christ's hands.

Name it.
Speak it.
Offer it.
Be Healed.

For Reflection:
- What parts of your story still need to be named?
- What have you avoided calling by its true name - and why?
- How might naming what happened help you move toward freedom?
- Read Genesis 2:18-20

20.   Healing Requires Safety

> "Come away by yourselves to a deserted place and
> rest a while."
>
> – Mark 6:31

You cannot heal a wound that is being reopened daily.
You cannot rebuild a house that is still on fire.
You cannot recover or discover your voice in a place where silence is demanded.

That sounds obvious. But for many Christians, the spiritual meaning is not.

Some Christians tend to stay in destructive environments because they have been told:
- "God hates divorce, so it is better to stay in an abusive relationship." (See the Appendix on more on this).
- "You're called to suffer with Christ."
- "Don't give up on people."
- "Jesus was betrayed too - so who are you to complain?"

These teachings are either deeply misapplied or weaponized.
And they lead to deep spiritual confusion, isolation, and trauma.

God Does Not Call You to Stay in Abuse
Let this be clear: God does not ask you to remain where you are actively being wounded.

Yes, God can bring good out of suffering. But that does not mean you must seek out suffering - or passively endure it forever.

The Cross was chosen by Christ for our salvation.

You did not choose the pain you experienced, and it does not redeem others by your remaining in it especially because it is against your better good.

Jesus told His disciples: "When they persecute you in one town, flee to the next." (Matthew 10:23)
He did not say: "Stay and let them destroy you."

Sometimes, holiness is staying.
Other times, it is leaving.

Healing Requires Safety

If your nervous system is in constant survival mode...
If you wake up afraid of what today might bring...
If you feel like you are walking on eggshells...
If you are constantly second-guessing your memory, your feelings, your worth...

That is not healing.
> That is managing trauma.

Healing begins when harm stops.
- When your body and spirit are no longer under daily threat.
- When truth is allowed to be spoken.
- When you are safe.

It's Not "Unforgiveness" to Leave

You can:
- Forgive your spouse - and separate until there is healing or divorce if all else fails.
- Forgive your parent - and go no contact for a time.
- Forgive your pastor or priest - and report him to Church authorities or go to another parish.
- Forgive your boss - and find a new job.
- Forgive your abuser - and still seek justice.

Forgiveness does not mean exposing yourself to further harm.
That is not mercy.
That is misused theology.

Jesus Withdrew - And So Can You

Jesus frequently left:
- He withdrew from crowds who tried to control Him.
- He slipped away when people plotted against Him.
- He escaped to the wilderness for prayer and recovery.

At no point did He allow others to manipulate, coerce, or control Him. Even knowing his silence would lead to His death, He reminds Pilate the He lays His life freely.

You are allowed to leave the people, systems, or relationships that continue to hurt you.
Not out of spite. Not out of bitterness.
But out of wisdom - and trust in God's desire to heal you.

But What About Martyrdom?
Some will say, "Aren't we supposed to take up our cross?"

Yes - but Christ never asks us to take up someone else's sin as if it were ours to carry.

Martyrs lay down their lives in freedom - not because they are trapped in cycles of abuse.

You are not failing the Gospel if you walk away from abuse.
You are refusing to let evil masquerade as holiness.

What Healing Needs
Healing requires:
- Time.
- Truth.
- Safety.
- Boundaries.
- Support.

And if your environment will not allow those things - you are allowed to find one that will.
God is not honored by your destruction.
He is glorified in your restoration.

God Desires Your Wholeness
You are not made to live half-alive.
You are not made to flinch at kindness or distrust love.
You are not made to carry trauma like a cross.

You were made to be free.
To love and be loved.
To live in the light.

And that begins by stepping away from the places that keep you in the dark.

For Reflection:
- What spaces or relationships are still re-wounding you?
- What have you told yourself about why you need to stay?
- What does it mean to give yourself permission to leave?
- Read Psalm 121:1-8

21. The Power of Truth

> "The truth will set you free."
>
> – John 8:32

One of the most harmful things we tell people - especially in Christian communities - is some version of this message: "Let it go. Stop dwelling on it. Move on."

Often, it is said with good intentions. A desire for peace. For closure. For comfort. But the result is almost always the same:

Silence. Shame. Suppressed pain.

The implication is clear:
- If you were really healed, you would not talk about it.
- If you had truly forgiven, you would not still feel anything.
- If you were holy, you would forget.

But that is not what Scripture teaches.
And it is certainly not what Christ models.

Jesus Never Pretended

After the Resurrection, Jesus did deny His wounds.
In fact, they were the proof of His identity.

When Thomas doubted, Jesus did not say, "Let's not talk about the Cross."
He said, "Put your finger here. Look at My hands. Touch My side."
His wounds were not signs of weakness. They were signs of glory.
Not erased - transformed.
And yours can be too.

What is Truth?

As Jesus stood before Pilate before His crucifixion, He declared that He had come to testify to the truth. Pilate famously responded with a question: "What is truth?" (John 18:38).

To readers of the Gospel according to John, the question borders on irony. Just chapters earlier, Jesus had proclaimed, "I am the way and the truth and the life" (John 14:6). Pilate, shaped by the Gentile world of Roman politics and philosophy, may have been echoing the relativistic skepticism of his time. But for us, the answer is essential - for all healing begins with truth.

Truth is the mind's conformity to reality - seeing things as they truly are, both the good and the evil. Ultimately, truth is not subjective or shifting. It is universal, objective, and binding on all people. There is no "my truth" or "your truth" if they depart from reality.

When we rightly perceive and speak the truth, we are anchored in what is real. And from there, we can act justly and love rightly. That is why truth matters. That is why it must be spoken. Because as Jesus taught, "You will know the truth, and the truth will set you free" (John 8:32).

Often attributed—without source—to St. Augustine, though its veracity is undeniable: "Truth is like a lion. You do not have to defend it. Let it loose, and it will defend itself." When we stay close to the truth, we are truly free.

Telling the Truth Is Not Bitterness
There is a false idea in many Christian circles that speaking about your pain means you have not healed.
That is a lie.

Truth-telling, at least to the proper people, is not bitterness.
- It is not gossip.
- It is not an attack.
- It is a form of witness.

When you name what happened - clearly, soberly, honestly - you are not dishonoring the Gospel. You are living it.

You are saying:
- "This is what evil tried to do."
- "This is how it hurt me."
- "This is what God is doing now."

That is not a grudge. That is testimony.

You are Not Crazy for Remembering

Trauma lodges itself deep in the body, mind, and soul. You do not choose flashbacks. You do not ask for triggers. You do not schedule nightmares or anxiety attacks.

But many survivors are made to feel ashamed for not "being over it."

They are told:
- "That was a long time ago."
- "You're too sensitive."
- "You need more faith."
- "Why are you still talking about this?"
- "You should forgive *and forget!*"

These responses do not bring healing.
They bring re-injury.

You are not weak for remembering (we are to forgive, but we do not need to forget, especially if there is danger of re-injury).
You are not faithless for still being affected.
You are not unforgiving for wanting the truth to be acknowledged.

Healing Requires Honesty

You cannot heal what you are not allowed to name.
Imagine breaking a leg and being told: "You need to walk on it. Don't dwell on the pain. It's in the past."

You would never recover. In fact, you would only injure yourself further.

Emotional and spiritual wounds are no different.

They require time, tenderness, and truth.

Honesty is not optional. It is essential.

The Cost of Pretending

When we pretend something did not happen:
- We isolate ourselves.
- We silence the parts of us that need attention.
- We protect those who harmed us instead of protecting those they may harm next.
- We train ourselves - and others - to distrust truth.

And worse: we keep evil hidden, which is where it thrives.

Scripture tells us to "expose the unfruitful works of darkness" (Ephesians 5:11). Not to conceal them. Not to make them easier to ignore.

Telling the Truth Is Healing
There is a holy power in saying:
- "I was hurt."
- "This was wrong."
- "I didn't deserve it."
- "I forgive them, but I will not protect their false reputation."
- "God is healing me - but it's a journey."

You do not need to shout.
You do not need to tell everyone.
But you do need to tell at least yourself the truth.

God does not ask you to cover evil.
He asks you to bring it into the light.
And when you do, He meets you there - not with judgment, but with mercy.

You're Allowed to Tell the Truth
Let this be your permission if no one has ever given it before:
- You are allowed to say it happened.
- You are allowed to say it hurt.
- You are allowed to say it still hurts.
- You are allowed to say you are healing, slowly, by grace.

That does not mean you are failing.
It means you are alive and healing.

For Reflection:
- What truth have you been afraid or ashamed to name?
- Who taught you to keep quiet?
- What would freedom look like if you spoke?
- Read John 14:1-6

22.   What Forgiveness Is Not

> "Then Peter came to Jesus and asked, 'Lord, how
> often must I forgive my brother who sins against
> me? As many as seven times?' Jesus said to him, 'I
> do not say seven times, but seventy-seven times.'"

> – Matthew 18:21–22

Forgiveness is central to the Christian life.
It is not optional.

But forgiveness is not what many people think it is.
- Forgiveness is not enabling.
- It is not pretending.
- It is not tolerating repeated harm.
- It is not trusting the unrepentant.
- It is not denying your pain.

And yet, Christians are often told - explicitly or implicitly - that to
forgive means exactly those things.
We confuse forgiveness with tolerance. And that confusion leads to
further injury.

What Forgiveness Is Not
Let us be clear about forgiveness. It is not:
- Approval of the sin.
- Excusing the offender.
- Avoiding consequences.
- Forgetting what happened.
- Reconciliation (though that may come later).
- Continued access or relationship.

Forgiveness is not naïve. It does not mean opening yourself up to more
damage or pretending someone is safe when they are not.

What Forgiveness Is
Forgiveness is the free and grace-filled decision, an act of the will, to
surrender the right to revenge. It is refusing to let bitterness rule your
heart. It is choosing not to repay evil with evil - but it is not pretending
the evil did not happen. It is choosing to love as God asks.
Forgiveness says:
- "I won't let what you did define me."

- "I release you into God's hands."
- "I will not seek to harm you - but I also will not protect your illusion."
- "I choose peace, but I do not owe you access."

Forgiveness happens in the heart of the one who is seeking to forgive. It is between you and God.

Forgiveness is a gift to yourself, and a gift to God. It is not necessarily a gift to the person who harmed you (though it can be if that person is the one seeking reconciliation). You do not forgive for the other's benefit, but your own. It is letting go of the poison that is hurting you.

It does not depend on the offender's apology, remorse, or repentance. In fact, the offender may not even be aware of you seeking to forgive. It is choosing to love them, even though they hurt you. That is what makes it powerful - but also, incredibly difficult.

Forgiveness Is Not the Same as Trust
Forgiveness can be immediate, but not all the time. Trust is earned and always takes time.

You can forgive someone while still:
- Keeping boundaries.
- Refraining to speak with them.
- Seeking legal or ecclesial justice.
- Protecting yourself and others.

Setting boundaries are not "unforgiveness." They are wisdom.

Jesus tells us to forgive endlessly - but He never tells us to tolerate evil endlessly.

"But Jesus Forgave Everyone…"
Yes, Jesus forgave - but He did not ignore sin. And not everyone was reconciled to Him, either, as He allowed them to reject Him, something we will address in another chapter.
He forgave the woman caught in adultery, and then said: "Go, and sin no more."
He healed the paralytic, then said: "Your sins are forgiven."

He spoke harshly to the Pharisees - because He loved them enough to tell the truth.
And on the Cross, He said: "Father, forgive them, for they know not what they do."

But those words were not permission. They were a plea for mercy - for a crowd who was still crucifying Him.

Jesus forgave, but He also suffered. His forgiveness did not erase the wound - it transformed it. He had a mercy with teeth.

Tolerance Is Not Mercy
We live in a culture that treats tolerance as the highest good. But tolerance without truth is not love - it is abandonment.

When we tolerate repeated evil without consequence, we:
- Enable the offender.
- Harm the survivor.
- Disfigure mercy into passivity.

Mercy is not ignoring justice or making it toothless. It is going beyond it - but never beneath it.

You cannot have mercy without truth.
And you cannot have healing without honesty.

Why This Matters
Many victims of abuse or trauma are told:
- "You have to forgive."
- "Let it go."
- "Move on, it's in the past."
- "Don't dwell on it – you have to love them like Jesus would."

Often, this advice is given too soon - or used as a shield to avoid addressing the actual harm. The result? More silence. More shame. More pain.

If you have heard these words and felt even more crushed, please know this: you are not crazy. You are not bitter because you want justice. You are not unholy because you still feel hurt or are angry over the injustice.

You are human. And forgiveness does <u>not</u> erase that.

True Forgiveness Liberates
Forgiveness, when rightly understood, is not a burden - it is a liberation. It means:
- You are no longer tied to what they did.
- Your identity is no longer "the one who was harmed."
- Your peace is no longer held hostage by their choices.
- You are not carrying their sin in your body or soul.

Forgiveness is not pretending evil did not happen. Forgiveness is a display of holy strength as it announces that the evil no longer can hide. Forgiveness boldly and prophetically declares that evil does not get the final word.

What If I Am Not Ready?
That is okay if you are not ready quite yet.

Forgiveness is always a process that begins with a series of deliberate acts of the will, not a single decision or feeling. It may begin as a prayer:
- "Lord, I want to forgive. Help my unwilling heart."
- "Jesus, I can't forgive yet. But I give You the hurt."

God is patient. He knows your wounds. He will not rush your healing.

You do not have to feel forgiving to begin forgiving. You only need to bring it to Christ.

You Can Forgive - and Still Tell the Truth
You can forgive - and still report the abuse.
You can forgive - and still warn others.
You can forgive - and still protect your boundaries.
You can forgive - and still grieve what was lost.
Forgiveness and truth are not enemies. They are allies in healing.

Letting God Judge

When we forgive, we are not saying, "It's fine."

We are saying, "God will deal with this - because I cannot."

We entrust justice to the One who sees all, knows all, and loves all.

He will not let evil go unaddressed. And He will not leave your pain unused. Nothing is wasted in the hands of the Redeemer.

For Reflection:

- How have you confused forgiveness with pretending?
- What boundaries do you feel guilty for wanting to set?
- What do you need to forgive - and what do you need to stop excusing?
- Luke 6:27-42

23. The Cost of Forgiveness

"Be kind to one another, compassionate, forgiving
one another as God has forgiven you in Christ."

– Ephesians 4:32

Once we understand that forgiveness is not tolerance or permission, we can begin to ask the next crucial question:
What does forgiveness actually require?
And as importantly:
What does it not require?

There is a great deal of confusion here - even among the devout. Many people carry spiritual guilt because they have been told that unless they have reconciled, forgotten, or moved on, they have not truly forgiven. Let us clear that up.

What Forgiveness Requires

1. A Willingness to Let Go of Revenge
Forgiveness begins with a decision: "I will not seek to return the pain you gave me."

This does not mean you do not feel anger or hurt. It means you entrust justice to God, and you refuse to feed hatred. It is a refusal to let bitterness become your master.

This is hard. Sometimes it takes repeated prayer. But this is the core of forgiveness. Eventually the anger and pain will diminish with the Lord's grace and time.

While pursuing forgiveness, keep in mind:
- You are not God.
- You are not the judge. You were not meant for that burden.
- That anger over the wrong is human. Give that anger to God and ask the Holy Spirit to purify it, heal you, restore what was stolen in His time.

2. An Honest Acknowledgment of the Offense
Forgiveness does not mean pretending you were not hurt.
In fact, real forgiveness requires that you name what was done. You do not heal from what you deny. You cannot forgive what you will not face.

103

True forgiveness looks evil in the eye and says, "You did this. It was wrong. And I release you into God's hands."

3. A Desire for the Offender's Redemption
Forgiveness does not necessarily mean you want the abuser back in your life immediately. It means you desire their salvation.

It is possible to pray for someone's conversion while keeping boundaries.
It is to say, "I don't hate you. I love you, and I want you to find God. But I cannot be with you at this time."

It eventually means that you would rejoice to see them in Heaven, free and forgiven, thanking God for showing mercy.

This is the mercy Jesus showed from the Cross - and the mercy we are invited into. A mercy with teeth.

What Forgiveness Does Not Require

1. Reconciliation
Reconciliation is a mutual process. Forgiveness can be one-sided.
You can forgive someone who:
- Does not acknowledge the harm.
- Does not apologize.
- Does not change.
- Has passed away.

Forgiveness is between you and God. Reconciliation is between people - and requires repentance, safety, and a shared commitment to truth.

2. Trust
You can forgive someone - and still not trust them.
In fact, it may be irresponsible to trust someone who is still unrepentant or unsafe. Trust must be earned through consistent honesty, humility, and accountability.

Forgiveness is free. Trust takes work and time.

3. Restored Relationship
Sometimes the relationship can be healed. Sometimes it cannot be.

Jesus tells us to forgive "seventy times seven" - but He also tells the disciples to shake the dust off their feet when they are rejected (Matthew 10:14). Regarding the unrepentant, St. Paul writes: "Avoid such people" (2 Timothy 3:5).

There is little virtue in remaining close to someone who refuses to stop harming you. Forgiveness does not require you to stay.

4. Immediate Emotional Peace
Some people feel relief after forgiving. Others feel nothing at all. That is okay.

Forgiveness is not always accompanied by a sense of closure. You may still feel grief, anger, or sadness. Those feelings are not signs of failure - they are signs of being human.

Healing takes time. Emotions take longer than decisions. Be patient with your soul.

Forgiveness and Justice
Forgiveness does not cancel the need for justice.
You can forgive someone and still:
-    Report them to authorities.
-    Testify in court.
-    Pursue accountability through Church or civil processes.
-    Set boundaries for the protection of others.

In fact, forgiving someone while still seeking justice can be an act of profound integrity. It means you are acting not out of vengeance, but out of love - for others, for the truth, and even, possibly, for the sinner's soul.

God is both merciful and just. So should we be.

The Witness of Forgiveness
Forgiveness, rightly understood, is one of the most powerful witnesses to the Gospel.

When you forgive - not by forgetting, not by excusing, but by choosing love over hate - you become an image of Christ Himself.

-   Not a doormat.
-   Not a denier.
-   But a disciple - who knows what was done and still chooses redemption.

The Wounds Remain - But They Are No Longer Ruling

Forgiveness does not erase that part of your story. It transforms it.

The scar may remain - but it no longer burns. The wound may shape you - but it no longer defines you.

It may seem that God's mercy and justice is slow, but God is the God of promises, and in His time, all will be healed. And in God's mercy, what once hurt you can become a source of healing for others.

For Reflection:
-   What pressure have you felt around how you are "supposed to" forgive?
-   What does healthy, God-honoring forgiveness look like for you now?
-   What are you releasing - and what are you holding accountable?
-   Read Luke 9:23-27

24. Justice and Mercy: Not Either/Or

> "He has shown you, O man, what is good; and what
> does the Lord require of you but to do justice, and to
> love mercy, and to walk humbly with your God?"

> – Micah 6:8

One of the most persistent spiritual confusions in Christian life is this: "If I want to show mercy, I have to give up on justice."

Or its painful cousin: "If I seek justice, I must not be very merciful."

This false divide has caused immeasurable harm. It has:
- Silenced survivors.
- Shielded abusers.
- Undermined trust in the Church.
- Confused the faithful.
- Fractured the soul.

But Scripture never teaches that mercy and justice are at odds. In fact, it teaches the opposite. God's justice and God's mercy are perfectly united - not in tension, but in harmony. St. Thomas Aquinas teaches that Mercy is not weakness; it is love's response to suffering - and includes justice. (*Summa Theologiae*, II-II q. 30, and 1, q. 21).

What Is Justice?
Justice is giving to each person what is rightly due. That includes:
- Truth.
- Accountability.
- Protection.
- Restitution.
- Correction.
- Restoration of dignity.

Justice is not revenge. It is not punishment for punishment's sake.
It is the rightful order of things, restored in love. Any punishment or consequence is to repair the damage done, at least in part, and demonstrate change.

What Is Mercy?

Mercy is the loving response to suffering and sin.

It seeks the good of the other, even when they do not deserve it.

It is patient, kind, redemptive.

Mercy does not erase consequences, but it may take them on or reduce them.

Mercy enters into pain with compassion - sometimes with correction, sometimes with comfort.

Mercy Without Justice Isn't Love

A mercy that avoids truth is not mercy.

A mercy that silences survivors is not mercy.

A mercy that allows continued harm is not mercy.

- It is cowardice.
- Or sentimentality.
- Or self-protection.

True mercy demands we take sin seriously - because sin wounds souls, destroys trust, and distorts love.

If you love someone, you do not excuse their abuse. You call them to repentance - for their sake and for the sake of those they have hurt.

God's mercy is never soft on evil. His justice is never toothless. Neither is His mercy. It has consequences.

It is tender with the sinner, but fierce in confronting sin.

Justice Without Mercy Isn't Holy

On the other hand, justice without mercy can become cold, harsh, and legalistic.

Mercy does not deny justice - but it transforms the way we pursue it.

- It seeks redemption, not destruction.
- It leaves room for grace.
- It never writes people off as too far gone.
- It holds truth and hope at the same time.
- It says, "You did this, and it matters - and I still desire your good."

The Cross Is Where They Meet

At the Cross, justice and mercy meet (Psalm 85:10).

Justice declares sin is real. It has consequences. The wages of sin is death.

Mercy declares that Christ lovingly takes those consequences upon Himself.

God does not wave sin away. He takes it seriously enough to suffer the punishment Himself.

That is not compromise. That is divine love.

You Can Seek Justice - and Still Be Merciful

If someone has harmed you, you are allowed to seek:
- Legal action.
- Accountability.
- Personal boundaries.
- Restitution or acknowledgment.

None of that makes you unforgiving.
It makes you honest. And faithful.

This is because justice:
- Names what happened.
- Honors your dignity.
- Exposes the pattern.
- Prevents further harm.
- Invites the sinner to conversion.

That is not incompatible with mercy. That is mercy's other side. Justice gives mercy its teeth to protect.

Mercy Is Not Merely "Letting It Go"

Mercy is not saying:
- "It's fine."
- "They meant well."
- "It's in the past."
- "God will handle it - so I don't need to, or I can ignore it."

Mercy requires letting go of hatred.
But it does not mean letting go of truth. Or accountability. Or boundaries.

Why This Matters

When mercy is divorced from justice:
- Victims are blamed for "not moving on."
- Abusers are coddled instead of corrected.
- Communities become unsafe.

- Christ is misrepresented.

When justice is divorced from mercy:
- We forget grace.
- We seek vengeance.
- We dehumanize others.
- We become hardened by pain.

Only together do they become healing.

God's Vision: Justice and Mercy Together

God does not say "choose." He says: "Do justice. Love mercy. Walk humbly" (Micah 6:8).

That is not a sequence or a multiple-choice question. It is a posture of all three simultaneously. A way of life.

You are not unmerciful for seeking justice.
You are not unjust for choosing mercy.
You are walking humbly the path of Christ - who did both, perfectly.

For Reflection:
- What have you been taught about justice in the Church?
- How do you see mercy and justice working together in your healing?
- What justice do you still long to see - and who are you entrusting it to?
- Micah 6:8 and Psalm 85

25.   When Mercy Bares Its Teeth

> "Love must be sincere. Hate what is evil; cling to
> what is good."
>
> – Romans 12:9

We tend to picture mercy as soft.
> Gentle. Kind. Quiet.
> A warm embrace. A whispered prayer. A second chance.

And yes - mercy can be all those things.

But true mercy is more than comfort.
- It is strong.
- It is sharp.
- It is fierce.
- It is firm.
- It is sincere.
- It is protective.
- It is rooted in the truth.

Mercy is not soft justice.
It is not sentimentality.
It is not false permission.

True mercy has teeth.

Mercy is willing to fight - for truth, for healing, for justice.
Because real mercy hates what is evil.

What Does "Mercy with Teeth" Look Like?
Mercy with teeth defends the vulnerable.
It names sin for what it is.
It confronts destructive behavior.
It says, "no more."
It removes access from abusers.
It reports predators, even when uncomfortable.
It does not flinch when safety or souls are at stake.

Mercy with teeth is not mean.
It is honest.

It is rooted in truth and love - not fear.
And it loves enough to act.

Mercy That Bites and Protects
I know this image is strong - maybe even jarring.
Anyone who has seen dogs fight knows the power of teeth:
They can tear, break, even kill.

And yet, those same teeth can carry a vulnerable pup with astonishing tenderness.

And countless nature documentaries have shown lionesses using their teeth for both furious fights and tender transport of their cubs.

This is the paradox of mercy with teeth.
It protects what is fragile.
-   It can confront and restore.
-   It holds the wounded gently - even as it holds the wrongdoer accountable without vengeance.

True mercy is not about punishment.
It is about protection, truth, and the possibility of repentance.

When lionesses or domestic dogs carry their young, the cubs or pups instinctively go limp, relaxing completely in trust. Ethologists (those who study animal behavior) call this the 'transport response'—a reflex wired into mammals to facilitate safe maternal carrying. (See Irenäus Eibl-Eibesfeldt "Ethology: The Biology of Behavior (1970).) And like a pup or cub, we should learn to relax in trust of the One who is carrying us.

Old Testament Concept of *Hesed* and Mercy
In the Old Testament, the Hebrew word *ḥesed* is often used to describe God's loving-kindness, mercy, and covenantal strength. It is a term that appears again and again in Scripture to convey not just emotional compassion, but active, faithful love—the kind that endures and defends.

In fact, in the previous chapter, we looked at the well-known verse from Micah:
"Do justice, love mercy, and walk humbly with your God." (Micah 6:8)

The word translated as "mercy" here is *hesed*.

There is no exact English equivalent for this theologically rich term, but we can describe it like this:
- It fights for the beloved
- It binds itself to justice
- It acts in faithful love
- It protects, defends, and remains

In other words:
> *Hesed* is mercy with teeth.

False Mercy Is Worse Than No Mercy
We often confuse mercy with avoidance:
- "Let's keep the peace."
- "Don't make waves."
- "Everyone sins."
- "We're all broken."

But these are counterfeits.
- They protect comfort, not people.
- They preserve appearances, not truth.
- They defend the system, not the suffering.

False mercy:
- Tells survivors to stay silent.
- Pushes for reconciliation without repentance.
- Shields predators from consequences.
- Enables cycles of harm.
- Calls cowardice "compassion."

It is not holy.
It is not kind.
It is not of Christ.

Jesus Was Mercy in the Flesh
Jesus healed the sick and forgave sinners.
But He also flipped tables and called out corruption.

He showed mercy to the woman caught in adultery - and said, "Go, and sin no more."

He forgave Peter - but rebuked him: "Get behind Me, Satan."
He loved the rich young man - but did not soften the call when He knew young man's heart loved his wealth more than he loved God: "Go, sell what you have."

Jesus did not use mercy to manipulate or avoid discomfort.
His mercy revealed truth, invited repentance, and protected the innocent.

That is mercy with teeth.

Mercy Without Strength Isn't Safe
If your "mercy" allows harm to continue, it is not mercy.
It is fear dressed in a halo.

True mercy must be:
- Grounded in truth.
- Informed by wisdom.
- Willing to say, "Enough."
- Directed by love, not guilt.

This is the kind of mercy that creates safety - spiritually, emotionally, and physically.

It is the mercy of a Good Shepherd who lays down His life,
Not the hireling who watches silently as wolves circle the flock.

Love Sometimes Says "No"
We forget that love does not always say "yes."

Sometimes love says:
- "This stops here."
- "I forgive you, but you are not safe."
- "You are loved, but you must face the consequences."
- "You may repent, but you may not return."
- "You are a child of God, but you may not continue as you were."

That is mercy with teeth.
- Not vindictive.
- Not cruel.

Mercy with teeth is clear. Clean. Necessary.

114

Why This Matters

Far too many Christians have been taught to remain in abusive relationships, toxic workplaces or institutions, or harmful environments in the name of mercy, some by clergy, friends or family.

They have been told - explicitly or implicitly - that leaving is more sinful than suffering.

And it leaves them:
- Spiritually exhausted.
- Emotionally broken.
- Isolated and confused.
- Wondering if they have failed by "not being merciful enough"

This must change.

Mercy is not weakness.
Mercy defends.
Mercy protects.
Mercy fights for the truth.

What If the Church Recovered This?

Imagine if every diocese, every parish, every household chose:
- Mercy will no longer mean silence.
- Mercy will no longer enable abuse or cover it up.
- Mercy will no longer sacrifice the vulnerable to protect appearances.
- Mercy will mean justice, truth, clarity, safety, and boundaries.

That would be a Church or home people run to, not from.

That would be mercy that actually serves the Gospel because it is the Gospel message at the core- the mercy of God saving His people.

The Mercy of the Cross

The Cross was not passive.

It was mercy in flesh and blood - facing evil head-on.
It did not minimize sin. It carried it.
It did not excuse betrayal. It redeemed it.

That is the mercy we are invited into.
- Not false peace.

- Not indulgence.
- Not avoidance.

But the fierce, faithful, freedom-making mercy of Jesus Christ.

For Reflection:
- Where have I mistaken silence or tolerance for mercy?
- Is there someone I need to show mercy to - with clarity, boundaries, or truth?
- Where do I need to receive Jesus' mercy with strength, not shame?
- Psalm 94

26. Holy Boundaries

> "Above all else, guard your heart, for it is the
> wellspring of life."
>
> – Proverbs 4:23

Many Christians struggle with boundaries.
We have been taught to:
- "Turn the other cheek."
- "Bear wrongs patiently."
- "Lay down our lives."
- "Forgive endlessly."

These are powerful commands - and absolutely central to Christian life. But too often, they are twisted into an unspoken rule:
"If you truly forgive, you'll stay close. You'll stay silent. You'll stay available."

That is not Christianity. That is codependency in a false religious clothing.

Boundaries are not unholy. They are not selfish. They are not un-Christlike.

They are wise, necessary, and - at times - God-ordained.

What Are Boundaries?
Boundaries are the God-given recognition of your own dignity, freedom, and responsibility, and placing limits that guard them.
- They define where your soul ends and another begins.
- They protect what is good.
- They clarify what you will and will not allow.
- They help you live with integrity.

A boundary says: "I love you. I forgive you. But I will not allow you to harm me - or others - again."

Boundaries set the consequences and allow you to find mercy, mercy with teeth. They are not about forcing how others behave, but rather, setting the expectations of how you will act should that boundary be truly threatened.

117

Jesus Had Boundaries

Jesus did not entrust Himself to everyone. In fact, Scripture tells us: "Jesus would not entrust Himself to them, because He knew all people. He did not need any testimony about mankind, for He knew what was in each person." (John 2:24–25)

He walked away from towns that rejected Him.

He withdrew from crowds when they demanded signs.

He allowed His followers to walk away when they could not accept His teaching (John 6)

He called out corrupt and hypocritical religious leaders without apology.

He remained silent when falsely accused.

Even after the Resurrection, Jesus did not appear to everyone. He chose when, how, and to whom He revealed Himself.

Boundaries are not a lack of love.

They are a form of love rooted in truth - ordered, discerning, and free.

Boundaries and Forgiveness

Forgiveness says, "I release you from vengeance."
Boundaries say, "But I still will not let you near until I feel safe with you."

These are not contradictory. They are complementary.
- You can forgive someone and block their number.
- You can forgive someone and avoid future conversation.
- You can forgive someone and report their behavior to authorities.
- You can forgive someone and choose never to be alone with them again.

Forgiveness is about your heart.
Boundaries are about your safety and calling.

What Boundaries Do

Boundaries:

- Protect your peace
- Preserve your purpose
- Limit access to your vulnerability
- Create space for clarity
- Encourage accountability in others

Boundaries do not punish. They protect - you, others, and even the offender - from further sin.

What Boundaries Are Not
They are not:
- An excuse for bitterness.
- A refusal to forgive.
- A wall to punish or manipulate.
- A weapon of pride or control.

If you are using boundaries to punish, they are no longer holy.
But if you are using them to protect what God has entrusted to you, they are sacred.

How to Set Boundaries as a Christian
- **Pray** - Invite the Holy Spirit into your discernment. Ask for clarity, not only comfort. Ask the Spirit to help define your boundary.
- **Be Clear** - With that clarity, define to yourself and others what is and is not okay. You do not need to explain endlessly or justify yourself.
- **Be Firm** - Boundaries invite pushback. People who benefitted from your lack of boundaries will resist them.
- **Be Consistent** - Do not move the line based on guilt or manipulation.
- **Seek Counsel** - Talk with a spiritual director, therapist, or trusted mentor to confirm you are acting in freedom, not fear.

Love Does Not Require Proximity
You can love someone from a distance.
You can pray for someone you never speak to again.
You can want someone's redemption without allowing them into your life.

Jesus laid down His life for sinners.

But He never told the sheep to cozy up to the wolf.
He never told the wounded to go back into harm's way.
He told them to be wise as serpents and innocent as doves (Matthew 10:16).

That includes boundaries.

You Are Allowed to Protect Yourself

This cannot be said enough.
If you have been told that loving someone who has been abusive means letting them stay in your life, hear this clearly:
- You are allowed to walk away.
- You are allowed to go no contact.
- You are allowed to report abuse.
- You are allowed to say, "I forgive you, but I will never be alone with you again."

That is not revenge.
That is not hatred.
That is not weakness.
That is wisdom.
And the Holy Spirit desires us to live in wisdom.

For Reflection:
- Where do you need to draw a boundary?
- What has kept you from doing it?
- How might boundaries actually honor God more than staying silent or exposed?
- Read John 6:1-15

27. Reconciliation Isn't Always Possible

"If possible, so far as it depends on you, live
peaceably with all."

– Romans 12:18

Reconciliation is a beautiful thing.

When it happens, it is a foretaste of heaven - restored relationship, renewed trust, forgiveness embraced on both sides.

But sometimes, reconciliation does not happen.

And here is what many Christians need to hear:
That does not mean you have failed.

Reconciliation Is a Two-Way Street
Forgiveness can be one-sided.
Reconciliation can never be.

Forgiveness happens in the heart. It requires only your consent.

Reconciliation happens in relationship. It requires:
- Forgiveness, mutual if needed
- Repentance
- Accountability
- Mutual safety
- Commitment to truth.

Without these, reconciliation is not only difficult - it is unsafe, and more than likely impossible.

What Happens When Only One Person Is Willing?
Many Christians are told, "You have to reconcile."

But what happens when:
- The offender denies they ever did anything wrong?
- They minimize the pain they caused?
- They call you divisive for speaking the truth?
- They want reconciliation without responsibility?
- They are unwilling to change?

In those cases, seeking reconciliation is not only impossible - it is unwise.

You can still forgive, in fact you must, again, for your sake. You can still pray for their redemption.

But you are not required to resume relationship or restore access without the other doing their own work. You may not be able to be reconciled until they are willing to be part of the solution.

Even Jesus Walked Away

Jesus did not reconcile with everyone because they refused to be reconciled to Him. They refused to repent.
- He walked away from towns that rejected Him.
- He remained silent before Herod.
- He confronted the Pharisees - and never chased after them.
- He warned His followers that division would come, even within families (Luke 12:51–53).

Christ is the embodiment of reconciliation. But He never forced it. He honored freedom.

And He respected boundaries - even when it broke His heart.

Scripture Supports the Possibility of Separation

Sometimes the most faithful thing you can do is walk away.
St. Paul wrote:
- "Avoid such people." (2 Timothy 3:5)
- "Expel the wicked person from among you." (1 Corinthians 5:13)
- "Warn a divisive person once, and then a second time. After that, have nothing to do with them." (Titus 3:10)

These are not commands for cruelty. They are instructions for clarity.

Sometimes reconciliation is impossible because:
- The other person refuses to recognize the truth.
- The abuser is not ready to change.
- There is no recognition of the harm.
- The wound is too deep to reopen for now.
- Safety cannot be assured.

122

God is calling you to move forward without them.
That is not failure.
That is discernment.

You Can Still Have Peace

Reconciliation is not the only path to peace for you.
Peace can come from:
- Setting boundaries.
- Letting go of guilt.
- Releasing the *fantasy* of thinking that the other person will "finally understand."
- Entrusting them to God.

You do not need their apology to heal.
You do not need their remorse to move forward.
You need Christ, who understands what it means to love people who reject you.

What If Others Judge You?

You may be told:
- "You should have tried harder."
- "You need to go back."
- "You're only being bitter."
- "A real Christian would reconcile."

But often those words come from people:
- Who do not know the whole story.
- Who believe, falsely, that they have a right to be the judge.
- Who want comfort more than justice.
- Who have never had to survive what you did.

Jesus knows the truth.
And He never judges you for protecting your soul if you are seeking truth and His Love.

Reconciliation in Heaven

There is one place where full reconciliation is promised: heaven.

There, the repentant will be restored. Every tear will be wiped away. All wounds will be healed.

The redeemed will be fully reconciled with each other, even if that reconciliation was not found in this life. For now, on this side of eternity, we walk with human limitations.

Sometimes we love best by letting go of our desire for reconciliation now.
Sometimes we forgive best by creating space between us and those who are not ready to repent.

Sometimes we reflect Christ most clearly by walking away from those who refuse to walk in truth.

Let Go of the Guilt
You are allowed to grieve what never healed.
You are allowed to stop trying to fix a relationship on your own.
You are allowed to release the weight of seeking someone else's repentance.
You do not need to carry the relationship alone.
You have done your part.
The rest is in God's hands, our Just Judge!

For Reflection:
- Have you been pressured to reconcile with someone who has not changed?
- What does peace look like without that relationship being restored?
- How can you honor your healing, even if reconciliation never comes?
- Read Romans 12:17-21

28. You're Not the Problem

"Woe to those who call evil good and good evil."

– Isaiah 5:20

If you have ever spoken up about mistreatment, trying to be truthful and in charity, you have likely heard some version of this response:
- "You're too sensitive."
- "You're exaggerating."
- "You're overreacting."
- "You're only bitter."
- "You've always been the problem."
- "Why do you always have to 'rock the boat'."

Eventually, after hearing it long enough, you might begin to believe it.
- Maybe I am the problem.
- Maybe I'm too much. Too dramatic. Too unforgiving. Too damaged.

Let me say this as clearly as I can:
You are not the problem if you are in the truth.

You may have problems. We all do. You may be healing from pain or struggling with your own reactions. That is human.

But the fact that someone mistreated you?
The fact that someone lied, controlled, manipulated, used, or abused you?
That is not on you.

Gaslighting Is Real - and Sinful
Gaslighting is when someone intentionally (or habitually) distorts reality to make you doubt your perception.
- They shift the blame.
- They rewrite the past.
- They make you feel crazy for noticing something is wrong.

You are told:
- "That never happened."
- "You're imagining things."
- "I would never say/do that."
- "You made me act that way."

- "You're always the problem in every relationship, aren't you?"

Gaslighting is not only unhealthy. It is a form of psychological and spiritual abuse.

And when done in God's name or by spiritual leaders - including deacons, priests, bishops - it becomes blasphemous.

They Make You the Villain So They Can Avoid Looking in the Mirror

If someone refuses to take responsibility for their behavior, the easiest path to placate their conscience is to blame the person who notices it.

This is why:
- Victims are often portrayed as "difficult."
- Whistleblowers are labeled "divisive."
- Survivors are described as "angry" or "unbalanced."

This tactic shifts the conversation from what happened to how you are reacting.

And suddenly, the story becomes about your tone, your timing, your healing process - not their sin.
- It is deflection.
- It is manipulation.
- And it is wrong.

This Isn't Only About You

If you have been gaslit, blamed, or labeled as the problem, know this: You are not alone.

This is the oldest trick in the book.
- Adam blamed Eve.
- Eve blamed the serpent.
- Cain blamed Abel.
- Saul blamed David.
- The Pharisees blamed Jesus.

Evil always looks for someone else to carry its shame.

It projects. It punishes the one holding the mirror.

And it calls the truth-teller "dangerous."

It Feels Personal - Because It's Meant To Be
When someone consistently paints you as the problem, you begin to internalize that narrative. It is meant to isolate you, shame you, and confuse you.

But here is the truth:
- Naming evil is not a personality flaw.
- Setting boundaries is not un-Christian.
- Reacting reasonably to trauma is not overreacting.
- Asking for accountability is not unforgiveness.
- Feeling anger is not sin.

So long as the truth is with you:
- You are not unstable.
- You are not dangerous.
- You are not the villain for wanting truth, safety, or healing.

What If You Have Reacted Poorly?
Sometimes survivors feel guilty because they lashed out, shut down, or said things they regret. That does not always mean they were the abuser. It sometimes means they were trying to survive something they were never meant to endure.

Sinful reactions do not make you the cause, though your own sin needs addressing and healing.

You can be hurt and still hurting. You can be wounded, and still in need of grace.

That does not erase the original injustice.
Name your sin, yes. Confess it.
But never carry someone else's sin. Their sin is not your responsibility.

The Enemy Wants You to Believe the Problem is You
If Satan can convince you that you are the problem, he wins twice:
You carry the guilt of someone else's sin.
You stop speaking, protecting, or resisting.
- Silence serves him.
- Shame serves him.

-   Confusion serves him.

Clarity, truth, and freedom do not.
That is why this chapter matters.

Let the Lies Burn

Maybe someone said:
-   "You'll never be good enough."
-   "Everyone leaves you eventually."
-   "This is why no one likes you."
-   "God is disappointed in you."
-   "This is all your fault."

Let those words burn away.
-   They are not from God.
-   They are not prophecy.
-   They are not truth.

God's voice speaks healing, not humiliation.
-   Correction, not condemnation.
-   Conviction, not confusion.

You're Not the Problem - You're the Target

If evil has tried to silence you, it is likely because your voice is dangerous to darkness.

If lies have surrounded you, it may be because the truth you know is powerful.

And if you have been told again and again that you are the problem - it is because someone did not want to deal with what they did or what happened.

You do not need to be perfect to deserve healing.
You do not need to be silent to be holy.
You do not need to carry what Christ already died to take.
You are not the problem.
You are beloved.
You are a child of the King of Kings.
You are healing.
You are coming back to life.

For Reflection:
- Where have you been blamed for the harm you endured?
- What lies about yourself have you carried because of that blame?
- What truths need to take root in your heart now?
- Read Isaiah 5:18-25

29. Silence Hides – Truth Reveals

> "Have nothing to do with the fruitless deeds of
> darkness, but rather expose them."
>
> – Ephesians 5:11

When you finally find the courage to speak up and tell the truth - about abuse, betrayal, manipulation, or injustice - you may hear things like:
- "Don't be divisive."
- "You're tearing the family apart."
- "Why are you trying to ruin their life?"
- "Let it go - it's in the past."
- "Talking about this isn't helping anyone."
- "This will damage the Church's witness."

What they really mean is:
- "You're revealing the truth and it is making us uncomfortable."
- "We'd rather preserve the illusion than deal with the pain."

But here is the truth:
> Speaking up is not what divides. Sin is what divides and will as long as there is silence.

Charity Without Truth

People often blame the whistleblower or truth-teller for the fracture, forgetting the fracture was already there.

Silence did not heal it.
> It concealed it.

You did not cause the wound.
> You are only refusing to cover it up.

Telling the truth does not destroy unity.
> It creates it.

Pope Benedict XVI wrote in his encyclical Caritas in Veritate, §3: "Charity without truth would be more or less blind." And I might add, toothless.

The Good Shepherd Hears

Even as the sheep know the shepherds voice, the shepherd can recognize his sheep's.

When we speak the truth, we are calling out to the One who is Truth. And He hears us.

That frightens those that would attack.

They want silence, and especially you to be silent, so they can continue their attack.

So keep crying out.

The Good Shepherd hears!

Jesus Was Accused of Being Divisive

Jesus did not keep quiet to maintain appearances.

He exposed sin.

He called out abuse.

He disrupted false peace.

And what happened?
-   The Pharisees called Him dangerous.
-   The crowds turned against Him.
-   His own disciples tried to silence or correct Him.
-   He was labeled a threat to the religious system.

Sound familiar?

Jesus was divisive - because He told the truth in a world that loved shadows.

False Unity Is Not Holiness

Unity without honesty is fragile and false.

It is the kind of unity that:
-   Protects abusers.
-   Silences survivors.
-   Rewards image over integrity.
-   Enables generations of pain.

That is not unity. That is complicity.

True unity comes from truth, repentance, and justice - not mutual silence.

132

You're Not the One Breaking the Peace

Peace built on secrecy is not peace.
> It is a prison.

When you speak up, you are not breaking the peace.
> You are naming the war that has been raging under the surface.
> You are not creating conflict but identifying it.
> You are refusing to pretend it is not already there.

But What If People Turn Against You?

Sometimes they will turn against you.
- Because they are afraid.
- Because they are enmeshed with the abuser.
- Because your sharing of the truth threatens their comfort.
- Because they do not want to face their own silence.

That hurts. But it does not mean you are wrong.

And it does not mean you are alone.
Jesus stood alone.
So did the prophets.
So have countless saints, survivors, and truth-tellers.
You are in good company.

What Speaking Up Does

Speaking up:
- Breaks cycles of trauma and abuse.
- Shatters silence.
- Protects the vulnerable.
- Restores agency.
- Honors the God of truth.
- Declares, "This ends with me"
-

It is not about revenge.
It is not about attention.
It is about integrity, protection, and truth.

God Doesn't Ask You to Be Quiet

The God who called the prophets,
The God who wept over injustice,
The God who flipped tables,

The God who told hard truths,
The God who stood up for the woman caught in adultery,
That God is not asking you to protect false peace.
He is not asking you to preserve an abusive image of unity.
He is not asking you to protect reputations at the cost of souls.
He is asking you to walk in truth - even when it is costly.

You Are Not the Problem
Saying what happened in truth and love is not what breaks the Church.

What breaks the Church is:
- Abuse unaddressed.
- Sin protected.
- Victims silenced.
- Sinful leaders and people defended instead of corrected.

Your voice is not the danger.

The silence that preceded it was.

Speak - Even If You're Scared
You are not alone.
You are not crazy.
You are not the one who ruptured the story - you are the one brave enough to tell it.
And every time you speak, someone else finds the courage to stop hiding.
So speak.
>Even if you lose people.
>Even if you are called divisive.
>Even if they try to turn it all back on you.

You are not divisive.
You are telling the truth.
And the truth sets people free.

For Reflection:
- Where have you been silenced or shamed for telling the truth?
- Who accused you of "causing division" when you were actually revealing it?
- How can you honor the truth now, even when it costs something?
- Read Proverb 31:8-9

30. A Time to Speak

> Detraction and calumny destroy the reputation and honor of one's neighbor. Honor is the social witness given to human dignity, and everyone enjoys a natural right to the honor of his name and reputation and to respect. Thus, detraction and calumny offend against the virtues of justice and charity.
>
> – Catechism of the Catholic Church, ¶ 2479

Gossip is a poison that often passes unnoticed. Whether it is a lie or a salacious truth, it spreads quickly - and it wounds deeply. Gossip is a sin, and in Catholic moral teaching, it typically takes two primary forms:
- Calumny is telling a lie about someone to damage their reputation.
- Detraction is telling a damaging truth about someone who does not need to hear it.

Both are sins.

In civil law, the corresponding crime to gossip is slander (spoken) and libel (written). They are considered serious offenses when they cause reputational harm. Even so, if someone shares something they believe to be true, and they do so in good faith - not with malicious intent - it may not meet the legal definition of libel or slander. Intent to cause undue harm is key.

But in Catholic teaching, truth alone is not the only measure of whether we should speak. Both justice and charity must guide our words.

When It's Right to Speak
Calumny is always wrong. But sharing a painful truth is not detraction and can be morally justifiable if:
- The person hearing it has a right to know.
- The intention is justice, protection, or healing, not revenge.
- Silence would allow for harm to continue.
In those cases, it is not sin - it is necessary speech.

Ecclesiastes 3:7 tells us: "There is a time to be silent, and a time to speak."

Sometimes, silence protects injustice, and at other times it helps so that it is better heard at the right time when there is a greater possibility of justice. Sometimes, speaking out protects life or dignity, and at other times, might appear to be lashing out. It is a matter of justice to report abuse, corruption, or evil behavior - especially when others may be harmed by your silence. But the proper time and place and people need to be discerned.

This includes naming the abuser and the abuse, at least to the appropriate people: the authorities, those at risk, a therapist, or Church leaders. Truth spoken for the good of others is not detraction - it is charity and responsibility.

When to Stay Silent

Casual conversation, venting, or repeating details to those who have no need to know can quickly turn into gossip. It does more harm than good.

Before speaking about someone or something, especially if what you are sharing is painful, ask yourself to T.H.I.N.K.:
- **T** - Is it True? Is this from your direct experience, told to the best of your ability? Or is it free of hearsay or an opinion?
- **H** - Is it Helpful? Will sharing this assist, protect, or heal someone?
- **I** - Is it Inspiring? Is it meant to build up, bring to the light or justice?
- **N** - Is it Necessary? Does this person truly need to know this?
- **K** - Is it Kind? Is it ultimately seeking the good - of others, of the Church, of your own healing?

If you answer no to any of these, reconsider sharing in that setting. There may be another place, time, or person who is better suited to receive what you need to say.

When You're Seeking Help

It is always appropriate to seek support when you are hurting. Speaking with a trusted friend, spiritual director, confessor, or therapist can be part of your healing. But even there, examine your heart: are you speaking only to wound someone's reputation, to vent or complain without a desire for healing? Or are you genuinely seeking counsel, clarity, or healing?

We all need people to talk to. But not everyone needs to know everything. We quickly cross lines when we are only venting, seeking the other persons approval or sympathy, or something less than a deeper understanding of truth.

Who Needs to Know?
There are people who should always know about serious wrongdoing, especially abuse:
- Police or legal authorities.
- Church leaders or religious superiors (if applicable).
- Therapists or spiritual directors.
- Those who are in harm's way, or their guardians.

Telling the truth is not a sin when properly discerned. Telling it with love, justice, and clarity is often a work of mercy.

For Reflection:
- How has gossip hurt me or others around me?
- Have I been slow to speak fearing being accused of gossip?
- Have I experienced a time when to THINK before speaking might have helped?
- Read Ecclesiastes 3:1-11, 19-22

31. Holy Confrontation: Conflict, Mercy, and Making Peace

> "If your brother sins [against you], go and tell him
> his fault between you and him alone. If he listens to
> you, you have won over your brother."
>
> – Matthew 18:15

Conflict and confrontation are difficult - even for those who have already walked far along the road of healing. For many, the very idea of conflict can sound threatening. Confrontation may recall shouting matches, shame, manipulation, or abandonment.

And yet, if forgiveness is the work of the heart, then conflict resolution is often the work of the hands. It is where mercy meets truth and speaks.

Conflict itself is not sinful. It is part of living in a world of broken people - ourselves included. What matters is how we face conflict and why.

The False Peace of Conflict Avoidance
Many of us were taught, implicitly or explicitly, that good Christians should avoid conflict:
- "Keep the peace."
- "Don't cause trouble."
- "Be quiet. Smile. Endure."
But peacekeeping is not the same as peacemaking.

Peacekeeping is often silence dressed up as virtue. It *looks* holy but leaves wounds unhealed and truth untold. It avoids confrontation in the name of false mercy, but in the end, it enables injustice.

Jesus was not afraid of confrontation. He wept. He overturned tables. He rebuked those who harmed others.
And yet He never humiliated, dominated, or manipulated.

He told the truth in love. And when it was not received, He let them walk away.

We are invited to do the same.

When You Are Confronted

For those who have suffered abuse, both confronting and being confronted by someone who has harmed you may feel unsafe. Trauma responses are often trigger what is known as the Four Fs:

- Fight - arguing or reacting with emotional intensity, not truth.
- Flight - avoiding the situation or shutting down.
- Freeze - going silent or feeling paralyzed.
- Fawn - trying to appease the other at the expense of yourself.

These responses are understandable but are often unhealthy. Becoming aware of your default response can help you begin to heal it. Instead of reacting automatically, you can begin to respond intentionally.

Boundaries help you do this. For example:

- "I won't continue this conversation if you're yelling."
- "I need ten minutes to gather my thoughts before responding."

Clarity and calm can turn confrontation into a path of mercy.

When to Speak in Confrontation: Discernment and Courage

As we saw in the last chapter, Ecclesiastes reminds us, "There is a time to be silent and a time to speak" (3:7). The Holy Spirit will guide us in discerning that time.

Ask yourself:

- Will this conversation bring truth into the light?
- Am I seeking restoration or revenge?
- Have I prayed about this first?

If the answers point toward healing - not harm - it may be time to confront the wrongdoer.

It helps to imagine information that might lead to conflict like a moment of both rain and sun. Both parties might hold "true" experiences that seem contradictory. But like a cloudburst or sun-shower, the sun and rain can coexist. Conflict resolution can begin when there is a mutual recognition that both facts may be true, but only part of the truth. When each side acknowledges that seemingly contrary facts can point to a truth that allows for both, healing conversation begins.

Confrontation is most effective when both sides can discuss the matter calmly and without overly emotional language or blaming. Both need to desire to understand all sides of the truth, not just arguing from emotion. It also requires both to desire to find the truth, not just be right.

If emotions are too high, it is okay to pause the conversation, not to punish, but to create time and space for prayer and clarity. This is not the silent treatment. It is a boundary that will prevent the conversation from walking into dangerous territories, causing further harm or more deeply wound the already hurting relationship.

How to Speak the Truth in Love
Jesus gives us a model of confronting someone who has hurt us in Matthew 18:
1. **Go to the person privately** - Not in anger, not in public, but with love.
2. **Be clear and specific** - "When (this) happened, I felt..." Name the facts and the emotions without letting those emotions to override logic and reason. Be honest and do it without blaming or shaming. Keep it to the issue at hand, not some issue that may or may not be related.
3. **State what you need** - Not to control, but to invite.
4. **Be open to their side** - Conflict is rarely one-sided. Listen carefully. What are the facts they are protecting, and why.
5. **Set a boundary if needed** - If reconciliation is not possible, part in peace at least for a period of reflection.

You do not need to shout to be clear.
You do not need to justify your pain.
You simply need to stand in truth and let it speak.

You may find it necessary to take along another, not to gang up on the other, but as a witness. That person may notice something you overlooked or be able to help define the issues with more clarity.

And sometimes, even that will not work. Then, if there is no further way forward, you may need to walk away for a time.

When They Don't Listen
Some people will not receive correction. Some refuse to acknowledge harm. Others twist your words or dismiss your pain.

That does not make the truth invalid.

It just means reconciliation may not be possible, at least at this time.

Even then, you can forgive.
Even then, you can set boundaries.
Even then, you can walk away without bitterness.
Jesus let people walk away from Him you may be called to do the same.

See, in the model Jesus gave, the last step is to treat them as a sinner or gentile - not to abuse them but to pray and ask the Lord for their conversion.

Mercy With Teeth: Strength and Kindness

Holy confrontation is not about being harsh. It is about being real.
It is mercy that does not deny truth.
Compassion that does not tolerate injustice.
It is mercy with boundaries.
Mercy with strength. ·
Mercy with teeth.
You do not have to choose between being kind and being clear.
In fact, to be unclear is often to be unkind.
In Christ, you can be both clear and kind.

Reflection Questions
- What past conflicts have I avoided because I feared rejection, anger, or shame?
- Is there someone I feel called to speak with - not to accuse, but to invite to truth?
- How can I ask the Holy Spirit for courage, clarity, and love in conflict?
- Read Matthew 18:15-20

32. When A Loved One Does Not Believe You

The older son became angry, and when he refused to enter the house, his father came out and pleaded with him.

He said to his father in reply, 'Look, all these years I served you and not once did I disobey your orders; yet you never gave me even a young goat to feast on with my friends. But when your son returns who swallowed up your property with prostitutes, for him you slaughter the fattened calf.'

He said to him, 'My son, you are here with me always; everything I have is yours. But now we must celebrate and rejoice, because your brother was dead and has come to life again; he was lost and has been found.'"

– Luke 15:28-32

The story of the Prodigal Son is about many things - mercy, forgiveness, return - but it is also a story about misunderstanding and resentment within families. We already looked at the first half of the parable involving the younger son when we looked at apologies.

But the second half is just as powerful, if not more if we get the point. Often, though, the powerful point Jesus intends to make is overlooked because it is a little unsettling and unresolved. Remember He was addressing those who were self-righteous and criticized Him for eating with sinners. He wanted them to see they were the older son.

The older son does not rejoice in his brother's return. He does not even listen. He is angry. He feels overlooked and unseen. In a way, he expresses jealousy as he did not even get a goat from his father, never mind the fact that by law, when the father gave the inheritance to the younger son, he had to give it to the older son as well.

His bitterness blinds him to the miracle in front of him: his brother's return and reconciliation. He refuses to come in. And still - the father goes out to him. Again, the father is lavish in his love and invites him to the celebration. Jesus leaves the story unfinished: did he rejoice, or continue to pout outside in the dark?

When we looked at the first half of this beautiful parable, I called it the "so called Prodigal Son" because it was the father who was extravagant. But it also could be rightly the titled, Parable of the Two Lost Sons, as both sons were lost, one physically, the other emotionally and spiritually. That's the kind of lost that often hurts the most because one may not even recognize how lost they are.

This story reminds us that even in the midst of healing, not everyone will celebrate with us. And the opposite is true: in the midst of the wounding, not all will believe you.

When They Don't Believe You
Sometimes, the person who struggles with forgiveness is us. Other times, it is someone close to us - a sibling, a spouse, a parent - who does not believe our story, dismisses our pain, or tells us to "move on."

This can be even more painful than the original wound.

You may hear:
- "That didn't really happen."
- "You're being dramatic."
- "I never saw anything like that."
- "Let it go - it's been years."

This disbelief can be especially intense in dysfunctional families, where different children experienced remarkably different parenting. What one sibling saw as normal, another experienced as deeply wounding. Age, temperament, and proximity change everything.

But here is the truth:
> The fact that someone did not experience what you did does not mean you did not experience it.

You Don't Need Their Belief to Begin Healing
It would be beautiful if your loved ones affirmed you, listened deeply, and supported your healing. But if they do not, you are still allowed to tell your story, grieve your pain, and walk the path of healing. But:
- You do not need their belief to validate your memory.
- You do not need their permission to begin your recovery.
- You do not need to be dependent on their timeline to process what happened.

"If it is possible, as far as it depends on you, live at peace with everyone." (Romans 12:18)

Peace does not require absolute agreement on all matters. It requires truth, boundaries, love, trust, respect, and grace.

When They Were There - and Said Nothing
Sometimes the most painful experience is not disbelief, but inaction. When someone saw what happened, heard what was said, or witnessed the harm, and did nothing.

These are the hirelings Jesus warned about - the ones who flee or freeze when danger comes.

And now you may need to forgive them, too.

This does not mean excusing their silence. But it may mean reflecting:
- Were they hurting, too?
- Were they overwhelmed or emotionally shut down?
- Were they in denial, afraid, or under someone else's control?
- Have they forgotten or blocked the memory as a trauma response?

When the time is right, a gentle conversation - free of accusation - may open the door to healing. Or it may not. But either way, you are not powerless.

You Can Still Heal
Your loved one may never believe you. They may never validate your experience. They may never understand why you are still hurt.

But you can still heal.
If they believe you, that can open the door to shared healing. If they do not, it may be necessary to place that part of your story off-limits for now, especially if reopening it causes harm.

Either way, your experience remains real. God knows what happened. And you are not alone in the journey.

For Reflection:
- Am I okay with knowing others might not understand why we are hurting or seeking healing?
- Can I forgive those who seemingly did nothing to help me?
- Can I be more like the Father in the Lost Son story and just seek reconciliation?
- Read Psalm 55

33.   What If the Church Did Not Respond Well?

> The law of God entrusted to the Church is taught to
> the faithful as the way of life and truth. the faithful
> therefore have the right to be instructed in the divine
> saving precepts that purify judgment and, with grace,
> heal wounded human reason. They have the duty of
> observing the constitutions and decrees conveyed by
> the legitimate authority of the Church. Even if they
> concern disciplinary matters, these determinations
> call for docility in charity.
>
> – Catechism of the Catholic Church, ¶ 2037

These words may offer comfort to many - especially those who trust that the Church, as the steward of truth and grace, will always protect and heal. And that is what should happen.

But for some - especially survivors of abuse or injustice - this has not been their experience.
- Perhaps their confessor was dismissive or even implied that they were to blame.
- Perhaps a pastor or bishop offered no care, no protection, no follow-up.
- Perhaps the response was not pastoral at all - but institutional, more concerned with preserving the reputation of the Church than restoring the dignity of the wounded.

Maybe the survivor was pressured to return to an unsafe environment, was interrogated for unnecessary or overly personal details, or discouraged from telling their story - all under the pretense of avoiding detraction or "making things worse."

Some have been silenced, blamed, or gaslit.
Others have watched their abuser quietly reassigned, protected, or excused.

Some have had to carry their wounds alone.
For those who were victims of Sexual Abuse by Clergy or Religious, I have a special message in the Appendix "When the Abuser is a Priest or Religious."

When the Community Wounds You Too

It is not only leadership that can fail. Sometimes the community itself wounds.

In situations of divorce, abuse, or conflict, the community can take sides - often siding with the more popular, well-connected, or manipulative party. The one who has the louder voice or better image may receive sympathy or support, while the wounded are cast out, disbelieved, or left to feel re-victimized.

When the People of God - the very Body of Christ - fail to stand with the vulnerable, the pain is deep. And real.

You Are Not Required to Stay

It is okay to leave a parish if it is no longer spiritually safe or supportive. You are not abandoning the Church by walking away from a place that failed to uphold what the Church actually teaches.
You are not leaving Jesus by seeking a place where His presence is better reflected.

If needed, begin a new process of healing - this time for the wounds caused by bishops, priests, or fellow believers.

What You Can Do

You do not have to suffer in silence.
- If civil law was broken, report it to law enforcement.
- If Church law was violated, seek help from a trusted priest or canon lawyer to begin the process of accountability.
- If your soul is in turmoil, reach out to a therapist, spiritual director, or support group that understands trauma and faith.
- If your trust is broken, remember this: Christ is still trustworthy, even when His ministers fail.

When the Institution Fails, Christ Remains

The Church is both human and divine. It is holy in its sacraments, in its Head, and in its mission. But its human members - even its leaders - are fallible and sinful.

If you were failed by the Church, that was not Jesus failing you.

He still sees you.

He still weeps with you.
He still fights for justice.
And He is still calling you to heal, not despite your wounds, but through them.

Closing Encouragement
You have the right to expect truth, justice, and care from the Church.

If you did not receive it, your pain is valid. Your story matters. And your faith still has a future.

Please do not let the failings of the Church separate you from Christ and the Sacraments. Christ remains faithful - even when the local Church on earth does not.
And that may be the beginning of your healing.

For Reflection:
- Have I been hurt by the leaders of the Church that should have protected and provided me aid?
- Have the community members aided or hindered my journey to healing?
- How can I help others?
- Isaiah 61:1-3

34.　Some People Change. Some Don't.

"By their fruits you will know them."

– Matthew 7:20

Every story of healing longs for a moment of redemption:
- The apology that finally is offered.
- The abuser who suddenly realizes and repents.
- The family that listens and believes.
- The transformation that proves, "It was worth speaking up."

Sometimes, those moments come.
And when they do, they are sacred.
They are evidence of grace. They are reason to rejoice.

But sometimes... they do not come.
And that does not mean you failed.

You Cannot Change Someone Who Does Not Want To
You cannot:
- Convict them of their error or sin (that is the Holy Spirit's job).
- Make them see what they do not want to acknowledge.
- Force an apology.
- Heal their wounds.
- Rewrite their past.
- Carry their guilt.

You can:
- Pray.
- Speak the truth in love.
- Forgive.

But you cannot choose for them to change.

This is because change requires three things:
- Honesty.
- Humility.
- Desire to change.

Without all three, there is no lasting change - only performance.

Some people will show signs of repentance to regain access, power, or image.

But it fades when no one is watching.

True change is slow.

It shows up in consistency of deeds, not only words.

What If They Never Change?
If they refuse to change you bless and release them.
- You entrust them to God.
- You stop waiting for an apology that may never come.
- You stop trying to explain yourself to someone committed to misunderstanding you.

You stop seeking water from an empty well.

This is not giving up hope.
It is giving up control.

It is saying:
- "I can't change you."
- "I still forgive you."
- "But I won't let your refusal to change control my story anymore."

Letting Go Is Not Giving Up
Letting go is giving God the space to work.
It is stepping out of the way.
It is holding them in prayer for their conversion.
It is refusing to play Savior - or scapegoat.

Some people change.
Some do not.

Their change is not your responsibility.
Your healing does not depend on their transformation.

But Doesn't God Want Everyone to Change?

Yes, God desires repentance from all.

He can move the human heart in mighty ways. Consider St. Paul (Acts 9), as he was still breathing murderous threats, encountered the Risen Lord on the road to Damascus, and was forever irrevocably changed.

But God also honors free will.

Look at the rich young man - Jesus loved him, invited him, and let him walk away (Mark 10:17–22).

- Jesus did not chase him.
- Jesus did not force him.
- Jesus did not blame Himself.

Neither should you.

What About "Never Give Up on People"?

Love never gives up on people.

Not giving up might come to mean you forgive the person, and pray for their conversion. But you will not allow them to continue to hurt you.

But love also knows when to let go.

Some people use "don't give up on me" as a way to:

- Avoid accountability.
- Keep control.
- Delay real change.
- Exploit your compassion.

You can love someone deeply - and still step away.

Signs of Real Change

Real change is not often:

- Instant.
- Dramatic.

But it is never:

- Manipulative.
- Public only.

It is:

- Humble.
- Patient.
- Displayed even in private.

- Willing to listen without defending.
- Willing to act without being begged.
- Willing to lose privilege if that is what justice requires.

You will know them by their fruit - not their promises.

When They Do Change

When true change happens, it is miraculous.

It is messy, slow, painful, and worth celebrating.
- Reconciliation is possible.
- Restitution can begin.
- Relationship may even be rebuilt.

But even then, you are not required to reenter a relationship until trust is reestablished.

Repentance invites reconciliation - it does not demand it.

You are still allowed to set boundaries.

You are still allowed to protect yourself.

Honor Your Healing - No Matter Their Choice

If they change: praise God.
If they do not: praise God anyway.
Because either way - you are free by forgiving them.

Their repentance may never come.

But your healing is not waiting on them anymore.
Really, it was never in their power to control.
You have a God who makes all things new - even when people want to keep the old.

For Reflection:
- Who have you been waiting on to change?
- What would it mean to bless and release them?
- What freedom could begin if you stopped trying to carry someone else's repentance?
- Read Acts 9:1-20, Proverbs 13:20

35.   What If the One I Need to Forgive is Dead

> Death is the end of man's earthly pilgrimage, of the
> time of grace and mercy which God offers him so as
> to work out his earthly life in keeping with the
> divine plan, and to decide his ultimate destiny. ...
>
> – Catechism of the Catholic Church, ¶1013

Death marks the end of our earthly journey and the conclusion of our time to receive or reject God's grace. At death, a person's eternal destiny is sealed.

For those who die in unrepentant mortal sin – then irreparably separated from God's mercy - their fate is one of eternal loss, a separation beyond all earthly sorrow.

But for those who die in God's grace, having sought mercy, lived with humility, and forgiven others, the reward is beyond imagining: the joy of heaven and eternal communion with God. Even if that eternal happiness is delayed by the cleansing fires of Purgatory, there is the promise of eternity.

But What About Forgiveness?

What happens if the one you need to forgive - the one who harmed you - has died?

First, be at peace: your forgiveness, or lack thereof, does not determine their eternal destiny. That judgment belongs to God alone. And He is a Just Judge.

But your decision to forgive - or not - does affect you and your salvation.

In his book "Slaying Dragons," Charles Fraune recounts a statement from Fr. Ripperger, an exorcist:
"Everyone in heaven has forgiven everyone, but the opposite is the case in Hell."

That is worth pondering.

It may be that there are people in heaven who were never forgiven by others. But no one in heaven holds on to unforgiveness.

Forgiveness Is Still for You

You may never have heard an apology before the person's death.
You may still ache with questions and regret:
- Would we have reconciled?
- What could life have been like if healing had come sooner?
- Why didn't they change before it was too late?

These questions are part of grief. And when reconciliation is no longer possible in this life, that grief may feel even heavier.

But, as we have already seen, forgiveness does not require the other person's cooperation.
Even in death, you can still release what binds you.

Not to excuse.
Not to forget.
But to be free.

What You Can Do

Even if the one who harmed you is gone, there are still things you can do to move forward in healing:
- **Write a letter:** Name what was done. Name out your unmet needs. Express your desire to forgive. Then, when you are ready, burn it as an offering - or with the family's permission, place it in their grave or casket.
- **Have a Mass offered for their soul**. You do not have to feel it - you must ask God to do what only He can.
- **Pray a Rosary or healing prayer** for your own heart and that the experienced conversion before death.
- **Speak to a spiritual director or therapist** who can walk with you through the unresolved pain.

Healing Is Possible - Even Now

You will know you are moving toward healing when the thought of the possibility of heaven with them brings you peace, not panic.

If you are not there yet, that is okay. That does not mean that you are bad.
It only means your heart still needs time. And God is patient.

One Day, All Things Will Be Made New

You may never hear "I'm sorry."
You may never get the closure you hoped for.
But you can still forgive.

Because forgiveness does not change the past - it frees your future.
And God, who knows what you carry, will complete what He began in you.

Your story is not over.
Even if they are gone.
Even if it still hurts.
Even if you are not ready.
You are still healing.
And God is still with you.

For Reflection:
- Who do I need to forgive that has died?
- What concrete thing can I do to help me forgive them?
- How do I feel right now about the possibility of being with them for eternity?
- Read Wisdom 3:1-9

36. The Courage to Walk Away

> "By faith Abraham obeyed when he was called to go
> out… not knowing where he was going."

> – Hebrews 11:8

There comes a moment in many healing stories when the next step is not staying, or hoping, or explaining - it is leaving.
- Not out of bitterness.
- Not to punish.
- Not to prove anything.

But because your soul has outgrown what has been containing or contaminating it.

And walking away feels terrifying.
Because everything you have known is behind you.

And all that is ahead looks like fog.
But still, God is calling.

Sometimes, Staying Is What's Hurting You
You have tried:
- Praying harder.
- Forgiving again.
- Being more understanding.
- Shrinking yourself.
- Silencing your voice.
- Waiting for them to change.

But nothing changes.

And the truth becomes clear: You cannot become who God made you to be in a place that requires your silence to stay safe.

Walking Away Isn't Failure - It's Faith
Abraham did not leave because he hated his homeland.
He left because God was calling him forward to something better.

Jesus did not stay in every town.

He walked away from rejection, manipulation, and even the disciples at times. He walked away to continue His mission, to be with His Father in prayer. He did not always fulfill other people's expectations for him.

To walk away is not to give up.
It is to step toward freedom.

When we walk away, we are free from sin, but not free to sin.
If you are walking away from a spouse, you are not free to walk into the arms of another, at least without allowing the Church to look at the roots of your marriage (again, see the Appendix for more).

What Are You Walking Away From?
You might be leaving:
- An abusive spouse.
- A toxic parish or workplace.
- A manipulative parent.
- A distorted image of God.
- A community that loved the mask more than the real you.
- A system that protects the powerful but punishes the honest.

It is not always about physical distance alone.

Sometimes you walk away emotionally, spiritually, relationally.

But the decision is the same: "I will no longer participate in what's killing me."

It is mercy with teeth.

Why It Feels So Hard
This is sometime hard because you have been told:
- "Good Christians don't leave."
- "You're being dramatic."
- "This is how life is."
- "A little suffering never hurt anyone."
- "If you walk away, you'll be alone."

Those are not the voice of Christ.
They are the chains of fear.

Leaving Doesn't Mean You Don't Love Them

Sometimes we love people best from a distance.

Sometimes we honor our parents or siblings by refusing to be re-wounded by them.

Sometimes we love a spouse by refusing to enable their sin.

Sometimes we love the Church by exposing what is killing its witness.

Leaving does not mean you have stopped loving.

It means you have stopped sacrificing your soul to the false god of the illusion of peace.

You Can't Always Heal in the Same Place You Were Broken

Healing requires:
- Safety.
- Silence.
- Space.
- Truth.
- Support.
- Freedom.

And if your environment cannot offer those things, or others are actively working against them, then your healing may require departure. It is not an easy decision, but one that may be necessary.

You are not called to die slowly in order to prove your loyalty.

Christ died for you.

And you are called to live in Him.

What If You Don't Know Where You're Going?

That is okay. Neither did Abraham.

The first step is often the only one that is clear: "Not here. Not anymore."

God does not always show you the whole map.

He often gives you only enough light to take the next step (Psalm 119:105).

And He meets you on the road, in the wilderness, or wherever you may find yourself. And He may be sending others to help you.

You're Not Abandoning Them - You're Returning to Yourself

You are returning to:
- The you God created you to be.
- The you who does not need to beg for dignity.
- The you who can breathe again.
- The you who was never meant to carry their sin, shame, or silence.

Walking away is not abandoning others.
It is choosing to stop abandoning yourself,
especially if they have abandoned you.

Jesus Is Already Outside

Jesus is not in the power structures that perpetuate harm.

He is not in the broken system that people refuse to change.

He is not in the circle that turned against you.

Sometimes He is outside the gate. "Let us go to Him outside the camp, bearing the disgrace He bore." - Hebrews 13:13.
There, He is waiting.
Calling.

And He is not ashamed to walk with you.
You are allowed to walk away.
You are allowed to leave the place where you were breaking.
You are allowed to follow the Shepherd - even if no one else understands.
This is not a betrayal.
This is your Exodus.

For Reflection:
- What are you afraid to walk away from?
- What is the cost of staying?
- What would it look like to believe that Jesus is already outside the gate, waiting for you.
- Read Luke 9:1-6

37. When Others Walk Away

> As a result of this [teaching of the Bread of Life and
> the follower is to eat His Flesh and drink His blood],
> many [of] his disciples returned to their former way
> of life and no longer accompanied him.
>
> Jesus then said to the Twelve, "Do you also want to
> leave?" Simon Peter answered him, "Master, to
> whom shall we go? You have the words of eternal
> life. We have come to believe and are convinced that
> you are the Holy One of God."
>
> Jesus answered them, "Did I not choose you twelve?
> Yet is not one of you a devil?" He was referring to
> Judas, son of Simon the Iscariot; it was he who
> would betray him, one of the Twelve.
>
> – John 6:66-71

We have already explored the painful but necessary reality that
sometimes we need to walk away - from abuse, manipulation, or
spiritual harm - in order to pursue holiness and healing.

But what happens when others walk away from us?

The Ache of Abandonment
This may be one of the most painful wounds of all.

When people leave us - especially those we love - it can awaken deep
grief, fear, and shame. We might:
- Take it personally.
- Obsess over what went wrong.
- Try to force communication or chase closure.
- Vent to others or replay every conversation.

Or we might do the opposite:
- Shut down.
- Judge them harshly.
- Dismiss them to protect ourselves from pain.

The truth is often somewhere in between.

Jesus Understands

Notice what Jesus did when many of His followers left Him (especially John 6 in the Bread of Life Discourse or the rich young man):
> He let them go.

He did not soften His message.
He did not chase them down.
But you can sense His sorrow in the question He asks the Twelve: "Do you also want to leave?"

Even among those closest to Him, betrayal was present. Judas, one of the Twelve, would leave not only with his feet - but with his soul.

If Jesus was abandoned, misunderstood, and betrayed - we will be too. But like Him, we can respond with truth, grief, mercy, and peace.

What to Do When They Leave

- **Grieve honestly:** It is okay to feel the loss. Let yourself mourn. Do not deny it, but do not be defined by it either. Take it to God in prayer.
- **Examine your conscience:** If there is something you truly did wrong, own it. Offer a sincere apology - not a forced one, but one rooted in humility, accountability, and hope.
- **Do not force reconciliation:** Jesus did not force anyone to stay. Neither should we. Forced reconciliation only breeds resentment.
- **Pray for them**: Desire their good and release them to God.

This does not mean giving up on the person. It means giving up control. Let them be in God's hands.

Who Walks Away - and Why

Sometimes people leave us for reasons we do not fully understand. Other times, their behavior fits into patterns we have seen before. You may recognize some of these:

- **The Hirelings:** They were not malicious, only afraid or unequipped. They did not stand by you because they didn't know how. They may return one day - or they may not. Pray for them.
- **The Thieves:** They left because they could no longer take from you. Once you stopped being useful, they moved on. Some

leave because you have grown, and they were never interested in who you were becoming.
- **The Wolves:** They caused harm - and now that you have set boundaries or found strength, they are gone. Let them go. Especially when the wolf is a family member like a parent or child, it can hurt deeply. But it is better to lose a wolf than to lose yourself.

When it is your spouse, prayer might offer little comfort. If they left (quite often literally, not only disengaging), they demonstrate they may have been unwilling to give themselves or incapable of loving you as you deserve, and perhaps even failed to consent to the marriage sacrament. Despite the presumption of validity, perhaps the sacrament of marriage was not contracted in the first place. Without Sacramental grace, or the presumed full, free faithful gift of self, marriage becomes too difficult. Often, in retrospect, one may see that the attempt to 'make the marriage work" was one-sided.

This is a very painful realization, perhaps, but the tribunal process can bring healing and clarity. That is a gift of the process, if you choose to enter into it. As stated before, this harsh reality does not automatically free you to pursue other romantic relationships. I have included a separate discussion of this in the Appendix.

When the Rift Was Your Fault
If you are the one who caused harm, do not despair. Repentance is always possible.

Do the work and apologize:
- Name what you did without excuse.
- Acknowledge the pain.
- Offer a real plan for change.
- Respect the other person's pace and freedom.
- Even if they do not forgive immediately, do not give up hope. Healing and reconciliation may still come - but trust, once broken, takes time to rebuild.

Final Word
Sometimes people walk away because they misunderstand your healing. Sometimes they walk away because they cannot or will not face their own wounds.

Sometimes they walk away because they have chosen a different path altogether.

But none of these define your worth.

Jesus was abandoned.
Jesus was betrayed.
Jesus was left alone.
But He remained faithful - and rose again.

So will you.

For Reflection:
- Who has walked away from me?
- What pain or grief do I need allow the Lord to heal?
- Do I trust the Lord to bring healing and possible reconciliation in His time, or demand immediately? Why or why not?
- Read John 6:60-70

38. The Ones We Leave Behind

> The fourth commandment [Honor your father and
> mother.] is addressed expressly to children in their
> relationship to their father and mother, because this
> relationship is the most universal. It likewise
> concerns the ties of kinship between members of the
> extended family. It requires honor, affection, and
> gratitude toward elders and ancestors. Finally, it
> extends to the duties of pupils to teachers,
> employees to employers, subordinates to leaders,
> citizens to their country, and to those who administer
> or govern it. This commandment includes and
> presupposes the duties of parents, instructors,
> teachers, leaders, magistrates, those who govern, all
> who exercise authority over others or over a
> community of persons.
>
> – Catechism of The Catholic Church, ¶2199

When we walk away, separate, or set boundaries, we need to be aware of those we leave behind.

When we flee a wolf, we need to make sure that we do not become like the "hireling."
We cannot abandon the vulnerable.
We cannot betray our commitments to God or seeking the way of holiness.
When there are children in harms' way, we must still try to protect and provide for them.
When there are younger brothers or sisters, our example might help them, or if they are still minors, we might need to take extra caution.
Where there are coworkers, friends, or other acquittances, we will fail if we abandon them without warning.
When there is the potential of further harm, the admonition to not be silent is even more important.

Those we try to help may not understand.
They may not like us.
They may turn on us.

To avoid sin, you might choose to not share everything that you know, but you are issuing a strong warning of what information is needed to protect and inform them.

In the end, we aid those we can, those toward whom we have obligations. We live with our commitments.

We cannot force others into freedom. And we do not find freedom by neglecting obligations.
In the end, truth will reveal all.
But we must show mercy with teeth.

For Reflection:
- Who are the ones most vulnerable that I need to be attentive to?
- What if they refuse my help?
- Am I trying to live in freedom and truth? Or am I reaching for a false happiness?
- Read Luke 4:23-30

39. Spiritual Direction Helps Tell Your Story

> Now that very day two of them were going to a
> village seven miles from Jerusalem called Emmaus,
> and they were conversing about all the things that
> had occurred.
>
> And it happened that while they were conversing
> and debating, Jesus himself drew near and walked
> with them, but their eyes were prevented from
> recognizing him...
>
> – Luke 24:13–27

Imagine the sadness of Cleopas and his companion as they left Jerusalem on that first Easter Sunday. Their hopes and dreams of Jesus as the Messiah had been shattered. There was nothing left to do except go home.

A stranger approaches and walks with them. He enters their conversation, seemingly unaware of the events they discuss. Of all people, He knows them best.

You can almost hear the sorrow in their voices. The loss. The disillusionment. The confusion.

And yet Jesus draws it out of them. He invites them to speak of their pain. He listens. Then, gently, He helps them make sense of it. He shows them how all of it - the suffering, the betrayal, the death - was not meaningless, but part of a larger plan, one spelled out in the Scriptures.

We know the rest of the story. As He speaks, their hearts begin to burn. Hope is rekindled. They recognize the Resurrected Lord in the breaking of the bread - the Eucharist. And though it was evening, they immediately return to Jerusalem, transformed and eager to share the news.

The road to Emmaus is a powerful image of spiritual accompaniment. Jesus walks with them, listens to them, challenges them, and heals them. He does not rush their grief, but He also does not let them stay in despair.

A good spiritual director does the same.

They walk alongside you. They ask questions. They listen to your story - its joy, pain, confusion, and beauty - and help you begin to see how God may be at work in it.

A good director may challenge your assumptions or gently name a lack of trust. This is not to shame you, but to help you see where understanding or faith is missing. Their aim is never control but your freedom in Christ.

A wise spiritual director will listen with empathy, sharing only what is necessary of their own story, not to draw attention to themselves, but to offer hope. They reflect the heart of Jesus to you. They will be people of prayer, humility, and wisdom.

As St. Teresa of Avila is said to have taught, she preferred a wise director over a merely pious one. Holiness is essential, yes - but wisdom sees more clearly what God is doing.

Traits of a Trustworthy Spiritual Director

- **Sound theology:** If you are Catholic, seek a Catholic director trained or certified through a reputable program. Not all priests are trained in spiritual direction, but many know who is. Sadly, there are several programs that initially seem Catholic or Christian but embrace or promote New Age practices or Eastern religions. (Ask a trusted priest for a recommendation. A short list of trusted Catholic programs would include the Institute for Priestly Formation priestlyformation.org, the Avila Institute Avila-institute.com, or the Divine Mercy University divinemercy.edu.)
- **Living a sacramental life:** This may be difficult to discern immediately, but you have the right to ask. Obviously, a priest would be, but there are excellent lay spiritual directors and training programs.
- **Self-awareness:** They are attentive to their own psychological, physical, and spiritual well-being.

A Word of Caution

If a spiritual director:
- Dismisses your experience.
- Pressures you to reveal what you are not ready to share.
- Makes accusations or assumptions.

-    Or makes you feel unsafe or deeply uncomfortable.
You have every right to discontinue - even mid-session if necessary. Spiritual direction should be a space of trust and healing, not coercion or fear.

Reflection Questions
-    Have I ever experienced someone "walking with me" spiritually, like Jesus did on the road to Emmaus? What was healing or helpful about that encounter?
-    What part of my story still feels confusing, painful, or unresolved? What might it look like to let someone trustworthy help me make sense of it?
-    Am I open to spiritual direction - or have I had experiences that make me cautious?
-    How might I pray for discernment in finding someone who reflects Christ's presence?
-    Read Luke 24:13-35

40.   A Safe Place: The Sacrament of Coming Home

> St. Peter's conversion after he had denied his master
> three times bears witness to this [need of
> conversion]. Jesus' look of infinite mercy drew tears
> of repentance from Peter and, after the Lord's
> resurrection, a threefold affirmation of love for him.
> (John 21:15-17) The second conversion also has a
> communitarian dimension, as is clear in the Lord's
> call to a whole Church: "Repent!"
>
> – Catechism of The Catholic Church, ¶1429

The Mystical Body of Christ is perfect. The Church on earth is called to reflect that perfection. But because she is made up of fallen and sinful members, that reflection is often blurred. The Church, like her members, is in constant need of conversion - not always from bad to good, but often from good to better. This is the reality of repentance: to take on the mind of Christ and to be holy as He is holy.

Christ gives us two Sacraments of Healing we can receive after Baptism.

One is the Anointing of the Sick, which is typically offered in moments of serious illness or near death. It brings peace, comfort, and, sometimes, physical healing - but always spiritual healing and grace. Families are comforted, relationships often restored, and the soul is strengthened to face suffering with hope. Fear gives way to peace.

The other, sometimes forgotten or often feared, is the Sacrament of Reconciliation. This is the ordinary yet beautiful way that the Lord left us to find His forgiveness - in fact it was the first Sacrament He imparted after His resurrection. As He breathed on them, imparting the Holy Spirit, He said, "Whose sins you forgive are forgiven them" (John 20:22).

This sacrament reconciles us to God, who always desires to forgive and restore us to right relationship with Him. It is also called Confession, because we name our sins aloud, stating that we failed in thought or words or deeds, as well as the good we failed to do. As mentioned earlier, naming things robs them of their power. Especially in this Sacrament, naming sin becomes a source of healing. The Sacrament is also known as Penance because it invites us to repair what was damaged and grow in virtue.

Together, these names show the beauty of this sacrament: truth, healing, and return. It too moves us from fear to peace.

Some people are hesitant to go to Confession because they fear being judged by the priest, or they worry that their sins will be too shocking, too shameful, or too much to say aloud. But the truth is, after the first few months of hearing confessions, there are very few surprises for a seasoned priest. Sin, frankly, is predictable - sometimes even boring.

What is not boring is grace.

What excites the heart of a priest - and what stirs heaven - is when a soul reaches out for God. That is what a confessor remembers, not the details of your sins, but the beauty of your return to the Father.

And speaking practically: priests hear so many confessions that it is simply not possible to remember every individual or their sin. More importantly, priests are bound by the Seal of Confession - a sacred, absolute vow never to reveal what is shared in the sacrament. Breaking that seal carries automatic excommunication and removal from priestly ministry, and the Vatican has never reinstated a priest who has violated it.

Personally, I believe God gives confessors the grace of forgetfulness. I am not alone in this belief. This grace of forgetfulness is truly right because when you humbly confess your sins, God Himself forgets them. "As far as the east is from the west, so far has He removed our sins from us" (Psalm 103:12).

In fact, there is an often told story of St. Margaret Mary Alacoque. In 1672, she started receiving visions of our Lord, who revealed His Sacred Heart to her. Her spiritual director Father Claude La Colombière was legitimately skeptical, so he asked her to ask our Lord about the last mortal sin she had confessed. In obedience, she did. Our Lord replied, "I don't remember." That was proof to Father La Colombière. He was a wise spiritual director and was also canonized. He understood that when the priest says the words of Absolution over a penitent who has sincerely confessed, Our Lord does not remember.

If our Lord forgets, why would He allow a priest to remember?

Remember that priests-confessors are also sinners who go to confess their sins. Those who go frequently themselves are often more compassionate, more understanding, more loving because they are looking for those qualities in the priests from whom they receive the Sacrament.

So do not be afraid. Mercy is waiting.

For Survivors of Abuse

For those who have been abused, especially by someone in spiritual authority, this sacrament can be especially difficult. Being abused is not a sin, but many survivors carry misplaced shame or guilt into the confessional.

Some may:
-   Feel panic or triggers when entering the confessional.
-   Fear they will be blamed or not believed.
-   Feel pressure to confess what was done to them, even though it is not their fault or guilt to carry.
-   Struggle with scrupulosity, believing that love must be earned - even from God. (See the chapter "The If Game" for more on scrupulosity).

These are not sins. And a compassionate, well-formed confessor will help you recognize that. A good priest will help a wounded soul encounter the mercy of God, not judgment or fear.

If your experience in the confessional has been painful or damaging, you are allowed to go elsewhere. You are free to seek out a different confessor, another parish, or a priest recommended by someone you trust. It is okay to ask others about their experience, not the content of their confession of course, but how they were received.

When More Time Is Needed

Confession lines can be short on time, and some wounds run deep. Many priests are willing to schedule a longer confession or spiritual conversation outside those times. If you are recently returning to the Church, or if your story is complex, setting aside dedicated time may be the best way forward.

If possible, a spiritual director can also help walk with you toward healing - outside of the sacrament, or in the Sacrament if he is a priest.

Tips for a Good Confession

The purpose of confession is freedom - freedom from sin, shame, and isolation. Here are a few ways to prepare well:

1. **Be prepared**: Examine your conscience ahead of time. Identify your sins and patterns. Do not worry if you confess the same types of sins repeatedly - that means you are still fighting. But also avoid confessing the same acts that you had already confessed – this is from scrupulosity. For example, if you stole something since your last confession, that should be confessed, but do not re-confess every theft you ever committed.
2. **Be prompt**: Arrive early. If you need more than a few minutes, ask to schedule another time.
3. **Be precise**: Avoid vague statements like "I broke the commandments." Say which ones, how, and how often (at least approximately).
4. **Be personal**: Confess your sins that you did or did not do, not how another persons' sins affected you. Explanations may be helpful but avoid excuses. And certainly do not confess other people's sins. Confession should be more like a good apology, trusting that the Lord is ready to forgive and reconcile.
5. **Be peaceful**: Trust that God has forgiven you. Do your penance and walk forward in grace. If you struggle with scrupulosity, re-read the section on it in the chapter on regret.

What to Confess

Too often, this sacrament focuses only on mortal sins (Grave matter, full knowledge, and full intent). When it comes this sacrament, however, confession of all sins, great and small, lead to even greater freedom and peace. While some confessors may not fully understand, it is helpful to address the patterns of sin. It helps to name the fears and anxieties that are underneath, or the root sins or wounds. Doing so helps to sort out where the need for growth or virtue is.

A Quick Examination of Conscience

Use one or more of the following guides to prepare your heart:

1. Have I fallen into any of the Seven Deadly Sins: Pride, Greed, Wrath, Envy, Lust, Gluttony, Sloth?

2. Have I kept the Ten Commandments
   - Have I loved God above all else?
   - Have I misused God's name or sacred things?
   - Have I kept Sundays and holy days holy?
   - Have I respected parents and lawful authority?
   - Have I harmed others by word or deed?
   - Have I been chaste according to my state in life?
   - Have I stolen or cheated?
   - Have I lied, gossiped, or spoken unjustly?
   - Have I entertained lust or impure thoughts?
   - Have I been jealous of others' possessions or success?

3. Have I sought to live and grow in the Theological & Cardinal Virtues: Faith, Hope, Love, Temperance, Justice, Fortitude, Prudence?

4. Have I accepted the Gifts of the Holy Spirit: Wisdom, Understanding, Counsel, Fortitude, Knowledge, Piety, Fear of the Lord?

5. Have I encouraged the growth of the Fruits of the Holy Spirit: Charity, Joy, Peace, Patience, Kindness, Goodness, Generosity, Gentleness, Faithfulness, Modesty, Self-control, Chastity?

6. Have I lived the Beatitudes (Matthew 5:1–12): Where have I failed to be poor in spirit, meek, merciful, or pure of heart?

7. Have I served Christ in the "least of these" (Matthew 25:31–46): Have I seen Christ in the poor, hungry, sick, or imprisoned - and acted?

How to Go to the Sacrament

- **Greeting**– The priest may begin with the Sign of the Cross and a short prayer.

- **State your context** - How long since your last confession? Are you married, single, divorced? Share anything relevant.

- **Confess your sins** - Simply, honestly, without excuses.

- **Receive advice and a penance** - The priest may offer insight or encouragement and assign a prayer or action.

- **Act of Contrition** - There are several Acts of Contrition, and any and all are appropriate. Even a spontaneous prayer with the admission of sin and asking the Lord's mercy is enough - in fact, it often shows true contrition. A common Act of Contrition is:
    - My God, I am sorry for my sins with all my heart. In choosing to do wrong and failing to do good, I have sinned against you whom I should love above all things. I firmly intend, with your help, to do penance, to sin no more, and to avoid whatever leads me to sin. Our Savior Jesus Christ suffered and died for us. In His name, my God, have mercy.

    - Or: Lord Jesus Christ, Son of God, have mercy on me a sinner.

- **Absolution** - The priest prays the words of forgiveness.

- **Conclusion** - A brief dismissal:
  Give thanks to the Lord for He is good… R. His mercy endures forever.
  The Lord has freed you from your sins, go in peace. R. Thanks be to God.

Tips for Growth

This great sacrament, when used well, can bring tremendous healing and growth in holiness. That is why most who are committed to both are frequently going to the Sacrament. The focus is not on the sin, but on grace. Many committed to growth and healing might go every month or quarter, for example. It is a good practice, no matter how frequently, to have a plan for the next celebration of the Sacrament when finishing the penance. It should be noted that the Church teaches that this Sacrament should be received at least once a year, especially to confess mortal sins.

Closing Note on Confession
Confession is not meant to be frightening. It is an encounter with Jesus Christ, who already knows your sins - and still wants to be near you.

When we confess, we step into the light. We declare that we are not our worst moments. We let grace win.

And the enemy, who thrives in silence and shame, loses again.

For Reflection:
- What has me most anxious or fearful of participating in the Sacrament of Reconciliation?
- How do I best prepare for my next confession?
- Am in prepared to find freedom in Christ in the ordinary way He left to receive His mercy?
- Read Psalm 51

41.   Your Story Isn't Over

> "The light shines in the darkness, and the darkness
> has not overcome it."
>
> – John 1:5

You have been through the fire.

You have seen what others pretend does not exist.

You have faced wolves, thieves, hirelings, silence, betrayal, and perhaps even your own breaking point.

You perhaps have walked away from people, places, or identities that once were your whole world.

Maybe you are tired. Wounded. Healing. Still unsure what comes next.

But hear me clearly:

Your story is not over.

You Are Still Here
You have survived what tried to undo you.
You have spoken when silence would have been easier.
You have named what others denied.
You have chosen truth over comfort.
You have taken steps - maybe small, maybe trembling - but real.
And that matters.
It means the darkness did not win.

God Doesn't Need a Clean Draft to Finish the Story
You do not need to be fully healed, fully forgiving, or fully "together" for God to keep working in your life.
He writes in blood, sweat, tears, and brokenness.
He starts where others stop.
He rebuilds on the wreckage.
He resurrects what was thought to be dead.
"He will give you beauty for ashes." (Isaiah 61:3)
Not in theory. Not only for other people.
For you.

You Are Not What Happened to You

You are not:
- The betrayal.
- The trauma.
- The silence.
- The damage.
- The mistake.
- The failure.
- The secret.
- A helpless victim, not anymore.

You are:
- A survivor.
- A truth-teller.
- A child of God.
- A temple of the Holy Spirit.
- A member of the Body of Christ.
- A story still being written.
- A life still full of purpose and promise.
- A soul still capable of joy.

Healing Is Not a Straight Line

There will be days when:
- You grieve when others celebrate.
- You cry for reasons you cannot explain.
- You struggle to trust - even God.
- You feel strong, only to feel shattered again.

That is not regression. That is healing.

You are not failing. You are recovering.
One step at a time.
One word of truth at a time.
One breath at a time.

Even as grief has stages - anger, denial, depression, bargaining, and acceptance - and is now understood not to be linear, so too are the stages of healing. You may move through waves of pain, moments of clarity, deep sorrow, or the ache of what was lost. What was lost: the relationship you hoped for, the life you thought you would have, or the person you thought someone was. Healing is not a straight path, and

184

like grief, you may never feel "finished" with it. But your heart may grow to hold it without breaking.

But if you invite the Lord into that process, you will find that healing begins to carry hope, not only hurt. Some days will be harder. Some will surprise you with peace. That is normal. No matter what, do not give up.

You're Bigger Than What Broke You
You are not doomed to relive the same patterns.
You are not destined to carry others' sins.
You are not too much.
You are not too late.
You are not too far gone.

There is more for you:
- More peace.
- More clarity.
- More strength.
- More joy.
- More purpose.
- A more abundant life.
- More of Christ.

And it begins right here. With this chapter. With this moment.

God Is Still Writing Your Story
Even now, in your silence, your sorrow, your small victories - God is working:
- When you forgive in secret.
- When you set one more holy boundary.
- When you breathe through the anxiety, resentment, or regret.
- When you walk away from the voice that used to control you.
- When you choose to hope, even if only for today or the present moment.

These are holy things.
They are not too small to Him.

They are precursors to your resurrection.

God Wants to Use Your Story

As you find healing, you may begin to see that healing ripple outward. Other hurting relationships may start to mend. The wounded may find in you a listening ear, a safe place, a hopeful witness.

God wants to turn your wound into a witness. Not because you are perfect, but because He is.
This is not something you have to orchestrate.
It is something you get to cooperate with.

It is not about platform, performance, or pressure.
It is about participating in Christ's work of making the world whole again - beginning with your corner of it.

Rejoice in that. Rest in that.
Praise Him for that.

This Is Not the End

There will be new relationships.
There will be safer communities.
There will be mornings without dread.
There will be laughter that does not feel foreign or forced.
There will be moments of peace that do not feel borrowed.

There will be a day you realize:
-   "I didn't only survive. I am alive." And hopefully, you will thrive!
-   Because that is what Christ came to give.
-   "I came that they may have life, and have it abundantly." (John 10:10)

Not in heaven only.
Now. Right Now!

One Final Word

To the one reading this who is still unsure if they are allowed to believe that:
-   You are allowed to want more.
-   You are allowed to hope again.
-   You are allowed to be tired - but not finished.
-   You are allowed to live.

Your story is not over.

God is not done.

The light still shines.

And you are still here.

That means everything is still possible, especially with God on your side. And He is calling you to something greater.

For Reflection:
- What part of you has felt too broken to keep going?
- Where are you still waiting for healing, joy, or justice?
- What would it mean to believe that God is not done yet?
- Read John 1:1-5, Isaiah 43:18

Part Four: The Safety of the Sheepfold
42. Finding Safety in the Sheepfold

> So Jesus said again, "Amen, amen, I say to you, I am
> the gate for the sheep. All who came [before me] are
> thieves and robbers, but the sheep did not listen to
> them. I am the gate. Whoever enters through me will
> be saved, and will come in and go out and find
> pasture.
>
> – John 10:7-9

In the first part of this book, we explored moral theology and the mystery of evil. In the second, we studied the characters from the Good Shepherd narrative. The third part brought us into the heart of suffering - examining wounds, mercy and justice. We walked the path of healing, and the long journey of forgiveness and reconciliation.

But there is another element in the Good Shepherd passage that deserves our attention: the sheepfold - a place of safety, of belonging, and of rest. And at the entrance of that sheepfold is Christ Himself, the gate.

He says plainly, "I am the gate. Whoever enters through me will be saved... and will find pasture." It is through Him - not around Him, not beside Him - that we enter into the kind of life for which we were made. Life in abundance.

And so, as we near the end of this journey together, I would like to turn our focus toward what this "abundant life" looks like - not just for us individually, but for us as a community.

If were to listen to one of my homilies, you might notice I sometimes struggle to keep things brief. My parishioners remind me of it lovingly (and often). But here, I want to be clear: I do not want to prolong the Homily or the Mass needlessly. In the same way, as I write this book, I do not wish to delay its conclusion. I want to invite you into the beginning of something more, bigger, better.

The next few chapters will sketch what healing and forgiveness can look like within the Church - in our families, friendships, parishes, and communities. In other words, what it looks like to live inside the sheepfold.

189

The sheepfold is not made up of perfect people. It is made up of:
- Those still healing.
- Those already healed.
- Repentant sinners.
- Growing saints.

It is communion.
It is shared life.
It is where mercy lives - not just in theory, but in action.

For those who have experienced abuse or trauma, I know that may sound like a fantasy - perhaps even a cruel one. Maybe you have never known a safe community. Maybe every "sheepfold" you have encountered had wolves inside it. If that is you, I understand why this might feel impossible.

But I want to tell you: it is not.

The sheepfold is real. The safety of Christ is real. And the Church - when she reflects her Shepherd - is a refuge, not a trap. It is made of people who have followed the Good Shepherd, responded to God's call with strength and mercy, and still help us. It is made of those who have gone before and modeled a life given so totally to the Lord. And it is made of those who are meek, seeking to live and grow in virtue, and act with true mercy.

Maybe part of the reason it is hard to see is because the pain is still raw. The wound still unhealed. The memory still too near. I do not want to rush you past that. But I do want to gently invite you to consider this: What if Christ wants to lead you not only out of danger, but into communion?

Not into perfection.
Not into a Church without flaws.
But into a people learning to love as He loves - strong, safe, merciful, and true.
He is still the Gate.
And the sheepfold is still open.

Reflection Questions:
- What has the "sheepfold" - the Church, community, or spiritual family - meant to me in the past? Has it been a place of safety, or pain? Or both?
- Where in my life do I sense Christ inviting me deeper into communion - not just with Him, but with others who are also on the journey of healing?
- What would it look like for me to take one step closer to the sheepfold - whether through prayer, community, sacrament, or service?
- Read Psalm 91

43. Blessed Mary, Our Mother of Mercy

> On the third day there was a wedding in Cana in
> Galilee, and the mother of Jesus was there. Jesus and
> his disciples were also invited to the wedding. When
> the wine ran short, the mother of Jesus said to him,
> "They have no wine." [And] Jesus said to her,
> "Woman, how does your concern affect me? My
> hour has not yet come." His mother said to the
> servers, "Do whatever he tells you."
>
> – John 2:1-5

The Virgin Mary, the Blessed Mother, first among the saints and Queen of Heaven, goes by countless titles - Mother of the Church, Mystical Rose, Virgin Most Powerful, Our Lady of Sorrows. She is also rightly called Mother of Mercy.

Why? Because she is the woman whom God chose to carry Mercy Himself into the world.

She was conceived without original sin, not by her own merit, but by what the Church calls prevenient grace - a grace that flows backwards from the Cross. God gave her this gift so she could be a pure vessel to bear His Son. And because she was preserved from sin, she was also preserved from its effects - pride, selfishness, and the desire to grasp rather than to receive.

Mary is the humble handmaid of the Lord whose yes - "Let it be done to me according to your word" - became the doorway through which salvation entered the world.

Her Magnificat: The Song of Holy Reversal
When Mary visits Elizabeth, pregnant with John the Baptist, she bursts forth into song - a song the Church now calls The Magnificat (Luke 1:46–55).
> "My soul proclaims the greatness of the Lord;
> my spirit rejoices in God my Savior…"

This is no gentle lullaby. It is a bold declaration of God's justice and mercy.
> "He has cast down the mighty from their thrones,
> and has lifted up the lowly.

He has filled the hungry with good things,
and the rich He has sent away empty."

The Magnificat is a proclamation that the God of mercy is also the God of reversal - He lifts the broken and humbles the proud. It is the song of a woman who knew her heart was to be pierced with suffering, who trusted, and who knows that God is faithful.

Mary becomes a model of holy strength. Her mercy is not passive. It is formed in prayer, rooted in humility, and courageous in the face of suffering.

The Mercy of Cana

At the wedding feast in Cana, Mary notices something small but significant: They have no wine. This might seem trivial to us, but in ancient Jewish culture, hospitality was sacred. To run out of wine would have brought shame on the family. Mary sees it and intervenes.

Jesus' reply might sound cold - "Woman, how does your concern affect me?" - but it is not a rejection. In calling her "Woman," He honors her as the New Eve. And when He says, "My hour has not yet come," He is revealing that any miracle He works will begin the road to the Cross.

Mary does not argue. She simply turns to the servants and says: "Do whatever He tells you."

And Jesus listens.
He changes water into wine - his first public miracle, at the intercession of His mother.

This is mercy. It sees the need. It speaks. It trusts. And it acts.

Her role as intercessor continues even in Heaven (see the Catechism of the Catholic Church ¶963-975).

A Personal Memory of Mercy

Years ago, I was called to aid someone in deep distress. She told her story, and I knew no answers would be sufficient. She had been wounded by so many men. She had a distrust of our Lord as a result.

Instead, I invited her to pray with me, inviting Mary to help her. She had a small plastic rosary - one of those pull-apart ones that glow in the dark - and I asked her to hold the crucifix in her hand. We prayed the Sorrowful Mystery of the Crucifixion.

As she reflected on Christ's suffering with the Blessed Mother, I reminded her that He was stripped, spat upon, and abused. He was mocked, rejected, and killed. He endured all of this - not only to save us, but to be with us in our own pain. He endured it for you. With you.

And I asked her to invite Mary into that place of pain with her.
To sit with her at the foot of her own cross.

By the end of our time together, I saw a visible shift. Her face softened. Her voice steadied. Light had entered it.

Most in Catholic ministry knows this simple fact: When invited, the Blessed Mother brings our Lord, who brings healing and peace.

Mary, a Mother Who Sweeps

In the wake of the abuse scandals that came to light in 2002 and 2003 - scandals that shattered trust in priests and in the institutions of the Church - I recognized profound pain in my heart in the hearts of so many of my brother priests. These were good men, faithful men, who were grieving not only the harm done to victims, but also the betrayal of the very priesthood to which they had given their lives.

Amid those painful days, someone shared an image that has stayed with me ever since. They had asked the Blessed Mother where she was in all this suffering. Was she weeping for her Son's wounded Church?

The response was powerful: She is not only weeping - but she is also sweeping.

Like a good mother in springtime, she was going from room to room, corner to corner, revealing what had long been hidden, brushing out the dust and debris of sin, clearing away all that defiled what belonged to her Son. She was cleansing His house - not with rage, but with mercy and resolve. This was not chaos; it was purification. A painful, necessary sweeping of the Church she loves.

Mary does not turn away from what is ugly. She draws close to the broken places. And she will not stop until the Bride of Christ is radiant again.

Mary, Mother of Mercy

This is Mary.
- She does not erase our pain in the name of her Son.
- She enters it with us as a loving mother would.
- She leads us to the Sheepfold of safety.
- She leads us to the Cross - because that is where her Son waits.
- She is silent strength. She is intercession. She is the mother of mercy.

She is the Mother who sees: "They have no wine."
And still says: "Do whatever He tells you."

Reflection Questions
- When have I experienced the quiet, strong presence of The Blessed Mother Mary in my life - perhaps through prayer, beauty, or comfort in suffering?
- What would it look like to invite The Blessed Mother Mary to walk with me into the harder places of my story?
- What part of The Magnificat resonates most with me right now - and why?
- Read Luke 1:46-55

44.   St. Joseph, Model of Mercy

> Joseph her husband, since he was a righteous man,
> yet unwilling to expose her to shame, decided to
> divorce her quietly.
>
> – Matthew 1:19

St. Joseph is experiencing a powerful resurgence in the spiritual life of the Church. From the humble prayers of St. André Bessette to recent papal writings, this quiet, holy, just man is finally being honored as he deserves. He is a model of mercy and justice, strength and gentleness, fatherhood, and fidelity.

Many others have written more eloquently than I, but I offer this simple meditation, based on the Litany of St Joseph.

The Just and Merciful Carpenter
In the quiet village of Nazareth, far from palaces or priestly courts, lived a man known not for titles, wealth, or eloquence - but for his hands and his heart. Yet he was the Renowned Offspring of David.

He was simply called "the carpenter."
A *tekton* - a craftsman, builder, a laborer who shaped the hard things of the earth into useful, even beautiful, things.

But Joseph's true greatness lay not in what he built with wood or stone, but in what he built with mercy, silence, trust, and obedience.
When he is first introduced in the Gospel of Matthew, we do not hear his voice. We hear of his character.

"Joseph, being a just man..."
In Jewish tradition, to be "just" (*tzaddik*) meant to follow the Law faithfully. But Joseph's justice was not rigid or punishing. It was the kind of justice that made room for mercy. When Mary was found with child, he had every legal right to expose her, to protect his own honor. But the Gospel says he was "unwilling to expose her to shame." He knew of her vow to the Lord to virginity and vowed to protect her. Walking away would have been understandable.

Even before the angel revealed the divine plan, Joseph had already chosen the way of compassion.

He would act quietly, protectively.
He would shoulder confusion and pain in silence, to spare her.
He would build, not with hammer and chisel, but with a father's courage
and a husband's reverence.

He would be Joseph most just,
       Joseph most chaste,
       Joseph most prudent,
       Joseph most obedient,
       Joseph most faithful -
he lived these virtues not in speeches, but in action.

And when the angel came, Joseph did not argue.
He rose - as he would do many times -
to take Mary into his home, becoming the Spouse of the Mother of God,
       to become the Foster Father of the Son of God
       to lead his family to Egypt, as a Diligent Protector of Christ
       to return and settle in Nazareth as Head of the Holy Family.

Always rising, always trusting, always silent.
       He became the Mirror of patience,
       Lover of poverty,
       Model of artisans,
       Glory of home life -

But in the eyes of his neighbors, Joseph was ordinary.

"Is not this the carpenter's son?"

They did not know that Joseph had formed the Son of God's hands,
teaching him how to work with calloused fingers, how to shape things
with care. They did not see that this "carpenter" had crafted a space for
the Incarnate Word to grow in peace.

He revealed he was:
       Chaste guardian of the Virgin,
       Guardian of virgins,
       Pillar of families,
       Solace of the wretched,
       Hope of the sick -

They did not know that the quiet justice of Joseph was the building for the early years of our salvation.

To the world, he was a mere carpenter.

But heaven knew: he was the Protector of Holy Church,
    the Terror of demons,
    and the Patron of the dying.

And the demons still tremble at the humility and mercy of this holy man.

Prayer
St. Joseph, just and merciful,
You chose the path of compassion over condemnation
And faith over fear.
By your example, teach us to be just and loving.
Help us to rise when God calls - quietly, obediently, and faithfully.
Ask your foster Son Jesus Christ to shape in us a heart like yours: firm, patient, and full of mercy.
Amen.

Reflection Questions:
- Where in my life am I called to choose mercy over pride or fear?
- How can I imitate Joseph's silence - not as passivity, but as trust?
- Who are the people I am called to protect, even when no one sees?
- Read Matthew 1:18-25

45.   We Are Not Alone

> Since we are surrounded by so great a cloud of
> witnesses, let us rid ourselves of every burden and
> sin that clings to us and persevere in running the race
> that lies before us while keeping our eyes fixed on
> Jesus, the leader and perfecter of faith. For the sake
> of the joy that lay before him he endured the cross,
> despising its shame, and has taken his seat at the
> right of the throne of God.
>
> – Hebrews 12:1-2

I love these verses.

A great cloud of witnesses, angels and saints - those who have gone before us and now live in the glory of Heaven - worshiping, watching, witnessing, and waiting for each of us to arrive home. I often wonder if the author of Hebrews had in mind the great arenas of the ancient world, like the Coliseum in Rome, possibly under construction at the time he was writing. Imagine the crowds, the spectacle.

And then imagine this: in walks another soul, welcomed into the eternal embrace of God our Heavenly Father. The crowd roars in joy, cheering another saint who has run the race and finished well.

To hear that crowd, to one day be there, is worth every struggle against sin and selfishness, every pain endured and healed, every right decision to love and forgive even when it hurt.

We will have eternity to worship God with them - and perhaps even share the stories of how He saved us. I believe that will be part of Heaven's praise: the telling and retelling of His mercy. At last, we will see it clearly. We will understand His permissive will. We will grasp what we now can only trust - that He has been good all along.

But this communion of saints is not a distant reality.

We are surrounded by this great cloud even now.
Silent, yes - but beautifully present.
And they are waiting to help.
You may have already glimpsed them.

- A sense of holiness in a moment of prayer.
- The quiet peace of a loved one's presence in your grief.
- A memory of something a holy person once taught you.

That is the communion of saints.

Saints Are More Than Statues and Stories

Throughout my life, I have come to love many saints. Each one has a story of redemption. Each one reminds me that God is real, that He is good, and that He wants us home with Him.

I often say I have many "saint-heroes."
And I do. Too many to count.
They are my friends in Heaven. And they are friends to you, too.

Throughout the writing of this book, I felt strengthened by many of their stories. I have already shared about the Blessed Mother and St, Joseph, and a few other saints, but there were many more, but included are:
- St. James the Greater who, with his brother St. John had holy fire, but needed the Lord to temper it.
- St. Peter tried so hard and sometimes failed, but never quit, and was our first pope.
- St. Paul was firm founder of community and preacher of the truth.
- St. Thomas who expressed doubt and faith, and proclaimed the Gospel to India, where he died in witness to the Resurrected Lord.
- St. John, the Beloved who loved the Lord, listened to His Sacred Heart, and stood in silent worship as our Lord was crucified.
- St. Monica bore the burden of an abusive husband and wayward son, St. Augustine, and never gave up.
- St. Augustine struggled against sin and lust and taught the love of God.
- St. Peter Damian courageously confronted corruption and abuse among priests and bishops.
- St. Catherine of Siena dared to write strong words of correction to the pope himself.
- St. Joan of Arc was betrayed by Church leaders and burned at the stake for her prophetic obedience to God's voice. Bold, faithful, and fierce in the face of injustice.

- St. Thomas More was martyred for refusing to betray his conscience and the Church during Henry VIII's reign. Gentle and brilliant, he remained faithful to God and truth over earthly favor.
- St. Ignatius of Loyola taught the discernment of spirits to help us grow in holiness. He founded the Jesuits to proclaim the truth.
- St. Francis Xavier, with zeal for souls, longed to preach repentance in the heart of the universities that, in his view, had forgotten eternity.
- St. Teresa of Avila reformed her community radically - embracing chastity, poverty, and obedience - and was persecuted for it by her own sisters.
- St. John of the Cross was imprisoned and beaten by his own religious brothers for his efforts at reforming the Carmelite order. He forgave, endured, and wrote some of the most profound mystical works of the Church.
- St. Francis de Sales wrestled with intense anger, and by God's grace, conquered it.
- St. Margaret Mary Alocoque received a vision of Jesus the Sacred Heart and revealed the love of God to a culture that was rigorist and fearful of God.
- St. Rita of Cascia, having lost her husband and sons to revenge, modeled heroic forgiveness.
- St. John Vianney was a simple priest and confessor, spending countless hours in the confessional every day, leading countless to deeper repentance.
- St. Eugene de Mazenod was a son of divorce and was ordained a priest (something that, at that time, took a papal dispensation because of his parents) and formed a community that serves the most abandoned.
- St. Damien of Molokai served and lived with lepers, enduring neglect from Church leaders and civil authorities. He spoke out until he himself contracted the disease and died among his people.
- St. Maria Goretti was attacked at age 11; she forgave her assailant before dying from her wounds. Years later, her attacker converted and attended her canonization.
- St. Pier Georgio Frassati who modeled the Beatitudes, supported the poor around him with his family's wealth, often in hidden ways, and died of polio, perhaps contracted from those he served.

- St. Josephine Bakhita was kidnapped and enslaved, her mistress leaving her body scarred with abuse - yet she would later call herself "fortunate."
- St. Faustina experienced the apparitions of our Lord as Divine Mercy and declared that the Lord is merciful.
- St. Edith Stein (St. Teresa Benedicta of the Cross) was a Jewish philosopher turned Carmelite nun; she boldly confronted the ideologies of her time and died in Auschwitz. She wrote deeply on the dignity of women and human suffering.
- St. Maximilian Kolbe gave his life in place of another prisoner at Auschwitz. His mercy was not passive - it was heroic, deliberate, and sacrificial in the face of evil.
- Bl. Jerzy Popiełuszko was Polish priest and martyr who preached truth and human dignity under communist oppression. His sermons were bold, and he was killed for speaking against injustice.
- St. Oscar Romero was the Archbishop of San Salvador who spoke boldly against political corruption and violence. He was shot while saying Mass for calling out injustice.
- Bl. Stanley Rother, a diocesan priest from Oklahoma, served the poor and indigenous in Guatemala during a time of civil violence. When death threats came, he returned anyway - saying, "The shepherd cannot run at the first sign of danger." He was martyred in his rectory for standing with his people in mercy and solidarity
- St. John Paul II - A holy pope that lived under communism, taught so much, and helped spread the message of Divine Mercy which was suppressed because of a mistranslation from the Polish. And this Polish pontiff confirmed its Catholicity.
- St. Carlos Acutis died at the age of 15, but displayed a profound love the Blessed Sacrament, and understood that his love of video games could be a source of temptation, so He limited his playing to a few hours a week. He created the first website cataloguing the Eucharistic Miracles from around the world (http://www.miracolieucaristici.org).

Every saint has a past. And yes, every sinner has a future.

Many were mistreated, even while serving Christ.
Some were betrayed by the very communities they loved.

Yet again and again, they chose mercy over vengeance and justice over silence.

They followed the Good Shepherd.
And now they cheer us on.

You're Not Alone
The saints formally recognized by the Church are not only examples of virtue. They are living members of the Body of Christ. They are with us. They want to help. They want to pray for you.

Do not be afraid to ask for their intercession.

Introduce yourself.
Tell them your story.
Ask for their prayers.
They have been where you are.
And they know the way Home.

Reflection Questions:
-   Which saint's story most resonates with your own journey - and why? Consider what their life teaches you about healing, courage, or faith.
-   In what areas of your life do you feel alone - and how might the Communion of Saints remind you that you are not? Invite one or two saints to "walk with you" in that area through prayer.
-   Not to be presumptuous, but when you become a saint - wonderfully redeemed - what part of your story would give God the most glory? Let that part be a place of gratitude or renewed trust today.
-   Read Revelation 21:9-27

46. Jesus With Skin On

> They (the community of believers) devoted
> themselves to the teaching of the apostles and to the
> communal life, to the breaking of the bread and to
> the prayers. Awe came upon everyone, and many
> wonders and signs were done through the apostles.
> All who believed were together and had all things in
> common; they would sell their property and
> possessions and divide them among all according to
> each one's need. Every day they devoted themselves
> to meeting together in the temple area and to
> breaking bread in their homes. They ate their meals
> with exultation and sincerity of heart, praising God
> and enjoying favor with all the people. And every
> day the Lord added to their number those who were
> being saved.

– Acts 2:42-45

The early Church lived in communion - not only spiritual communion, but tangible, daily, life-giving community. Imagine the joy of being so connected to others that all your true needs - spiritual, emotional, even material - were seen and shared. Together they worshipped, prayed, broke bread (the Eucharist), and learned from the apostles. Each person was known, recognized, and loved.

That is what the Church is supposed to look like.

We may not be asked today to sell all our property or live in one shared house - but the heart of the passage still speaks truth That we are
- Meant to live our faith in relationship.
- Worship together.
- Share what we have been given.
- Uplift and care for one another.
- Love one another.

Even in the midst of great suffering, such community brings glimmers of hope.

While the Communion of Saints offers a powerful spiritual connection - our friends in heaven interceding for us - there are moments when we need what a commonly told story of a young person, usually a girl who was afraid of a thunderstorm, is said to have asked for: "*Jesus with skin on.*"

We do not need a theology textbook.
We need presence. Protection. Someone who would stand beside us in the dark.

The child in the story named what we all long for: someone who will show up in the name of Christ - not necessarily to fix everything, but to love us right where we are.

Jesus With Skin On
There are people like that.
Men and women, young and old, who live the Gospel with their lives.
They do not only talk about mercy, healing, or compassion.
They are bringers of mercy, healing, and compassion to those around them.

They share the gifts and fruits of their relationship with God. They radiate the love of Christ by being present, faithful, and generous - especially when the world feels dark.

In a previous chapter, I shared the story of my sixth-grade teacher. When I was quietly crying at my desk, ashamed and unsure of how to explain the sadness, she simply said: "Sometimes people just feel sad and need to cry."

That sentence was small - but it gave me permission to feel. It affirmed my dignity. She did not lecture me or try to fix me. She saw me. In that moment, she was Jesus with skin on. I thank God I was able to thank her so many years later.

I think of my mother's parents who lived the sacrament of marriage with integrity and joy. They loved Jesus Christ and His Church. They prayed together, attended Mass, served their parish, and loved generously. As a child, I often visited them after school. I helped however I could - and they welcomed me in, every time.

When Grandma got cancer and died, Grandpa was heartbroken. But even in his grief, he made room for me. He let me help, let me be a grandson. And he loved me deeply. I only realized later how much he had done for me, how much he saw and affirmed me. He was Jesus with skin on - to me, and to so many others.

And there were others - many others - whose presence, words, or kindness were like candles along a dark road I was journeying. Their light may have been small, but it was enough for that next step. And together, the journey became so much clearer.

The Invitation
I hope your story includes many such people.
If you have not named them yet, I invite you to look again.
It might be a grandparent, a teacher, a friend, a coach, a neighbor.
They might not say much, but they see you, support you, are cheering for you.
Or maybe, without you knowing, they are protecting you from something else.

Have you thanked them? Have you thanked God for them?

But here is a greater invitation:
Now it is your turn.
Whether you are in the thick of healing or on the other side of it,
whether your heart still aches or has started to rejoice -
you can be Jesus with skin on for someone else.

You can listen. You can show up. You can speak words of truth and tenderness.
You can carry the mercy that has carried you - and pass it on.

You do not have to be perfect.
You only have to be willing.

Reflection Questions:
- Who has been "Jesus with skin on" in your life - someone who loved you in a time of need?
- Where might God be inviting you to be that presence for someone else?
- What does it look like to build a healing, Eucharistic community around you today?
- 1 John 4:7-19

47.   Meekness: Strength In Submission

Blessed are the meek, for they will inherit the land.

– Matthew 5:5

The Beatitudes are among the most paradoxical and powerful teachings in all of Scripture. At the very start of the Sermon on the Mount, Jesus speaks blessings over circumstances the world would never call "blessed": mourning, poverty of spirit, persecution, and hunger. He calls them *makarios* - blessed, happy, fortunate.

Do these states sound like happiness to you? They do not, at least not at first. But Jesus sees deeper.

Each beatitude names a holy poverty, an emptiness that turns us back to God. They are not ideal conditions - but they are honest ones. When we suffer, when we lack, when we hunger for righteousness or peace, we discover the truth: the world cannot fill us. Only God can.

That is the key to understanding the beatitudes. They are not prescriptions for pain. They are invitations to live with open hands, letting go of the illusions of control, self-sufficiency, or revenge - and to trust that the God who sees will also save.

But What About Meekness?
"Blessed are the meek."
This might be the most misunderstood of them all.

To modern ears, meekness sounds like weakness: passive, quiet, submissive, maybe even cowardly. We imagine someone spineless - a doormat or a church mouse.

But biblical meekness is anything but weak.

In the original Greek, the word for meek (*praus*) was often used to describe a war horse - a powerful, muscular animal, fully trained and under control. Not wild, not timid, but strong and focused. It could charge into battle and hold steady even in chaos. Why? Because it trusted its rider.

That is biblical meekness: Strength under control. Power surrendered to purpose. A soul anchored in God's will, not driven by its own.

This is what Jesus praised. This is what He modeled.

He who could silence storms and summon angels chose the path of meekness:

> "Take my yoke upon you and learn from me, for I
> am meek and humble of heart." (cf. Matthew 11:29)

Meekness in the Midst of the Battle

For those who have experienced trauma, injustice, or deep wounding, the idea of meekness may feel uncomfortable - even unsafe. Haven't we already been silenced, stepped on, or ignored? Aren't we finally learning to stand up for ourselves?

Yes - and that's precisely why biblical meekness matters.

Meekness is not denial of your strength.
It is the discipline to use your strength rightly.
In fact, meekness is living mercy and justice with teeth as they ought to be lived!

It is not silence in the face of evil - it is the ability to speak truth without rage, to confront injustice without becoming unjust, to be rooted so deeply in Christ that the winds of the world cannot uproot you.

Becoming Meek: Discipleship and Discipline

The word disciple shares a root with discipline. To become meek, we must be formed. Trained. Ordered toward God.

This means becoming students - disciples - of Jesus Christ, learning from His Sacred Heart, patterned by His mercy and mission. We are not the follower of a system of beliefs, but of the Person of Jesus Christ, invited into a personal, life-saving relationship. No other religion or philosophy offers such intimacy. Meekness allows us to be His disciples, and He makes us His friends. So Christ gave the Church to form disciples.

Christ gives the Church tools for our growth:

- The Holy Spirit, the Third Person of the Trinity, to dwell in us and guide us to Christ.
- The Sacraments, which give us grace:
  o Baptism makes us children of God.
  o Reconciliation restores us when we fall.
  o The Eucharist nourishes us.
  o Confirmation strengthens us with the Spirit and makes us full members of the Church.
  o Marriage and Holy Orders root us in vocations of service.
  o Anointing heals and prepares us to meet God.

And the Church, in her wisdom and maternal care, gives us countless means to grow in holiness, healing, and true strength:
- Sacred Scripture: The Church, under the guidance of the Holy Spirit, discerned and preserved the canon of both the Old and New Testaments, giving us the definitive Word of God to nourish our minds and hearts.
- The Liturgy: Especially the Holy Sacrifice of the Mass, where we encounter Christ truly present in the Eucharist. The Liturgy of the Hours, the daily rhythm of Psalms and prayers, sanctifies time and joins us to the universal Church in worship.
- The Rites of the Sacraments: Powerful channels of grace instituted by Christ for the imparting of grace - Baptism, Confirmation, Eucharist, Reconciliation, Anointing of the Sick, Matrimony, and Holy Orders - each a concrete encounter with the living God. The Church, in obedience to Christ gives us the way to celebrate these grace-giving Sacraments, setting both form and matter, words and functions.
- Sacramentals: Physical signs that prepare us to receive grace - such as holy water, crucifixes, rosaries, blessed salt, scapulars, and medals - which remind us of God's presence and invite prayer and reverence.
- The Catechism of the Catholic Church: A rich summary of our faith, drawing from Scripture, Tradition, and the Magisterium to teach clearly what we believe and how we are to live.
- Canon Law: The Code of Canon Law offers structure and justice to the life of the Church, ensuring order, protection of rights, and the common good.
- The formal process to recognize those we can trust are already enjoying the Communion of Saints: Not only do we honor and venerate the saints; we are invited to ask for their intercession

and follow their example. These heavenly friends walk with us in our daily lives. The Church declares them as acceptable models of holiness.

- Devotions and Litanies: From the Rosary to the Divine Mercy Chaplet, from the Stations of the Cross to litanies of the saints, the Church gives us beautiful ways to pray with the heart and reflect on Christ's love.
- Spiritual Reading and the Lives of the Saints: The writings of the Church Fathers, Doctors of the Church, mystics, and modern saints provide a treasury of wisdom for the soul.
- Magisterial Teaching: Through the guidance of the Pope and bishops in union with him, the Church continues to teach faithfully in every generation, helping us navigate the challenges of our time with clarity and fidelity.
- Retreats, pilgrimages, missions, and spiritual direction: The Church fosters sacred moments of encounter and growth, encouraging us to pause, reflect, and respond to God's ongoing work in our lives.

The Inheritance of the Meek
Jesus promises that the meek "will inherit the land."

This is not only about geography. It is about belonging. It is finding home.

The meek will receive the Kingdom - not because they fought for it, but because they trusted the King.

In a world where strength is too often misused - where power corrupts and pride wounds - meekness is a quiet revolution. It stands tall, but not proud. It bows but is not broken. It endures but never becomes bitter.
It looks like Christ.
And in Him, we find our true strength.

Reflection Questions:
- Where have I mistaken meekness for weakness?
- What areas of my life need more discipline or surrender to Christ?
- How can I grow in strength under control, using my power for truth and love?
- Read Matthew 11:25-30

214

48. The Spirit Poured Out: Strength for the Journey

> "The Spirit too comes to the aid of our weakness; for we do not know how to pray as we ought, but the Spirit Himself intercedes with inexpressible groanings."
>
> – Romans 8:26

The Christian life is not meant to be lived alone - or by our own strength. Healing, forgiveness, mercy, even faith itself - all of it is sustained by the Holy Spirit.

Even before His Resurrection, Jesus promised to send an Advocate, a Helper. And at Pentecost (Acts 2), that promise was fulfilled. The fearful became bold. The broken became brave. The disciples, once hidden behind locked doors in fear, went out to proclaim the Gospel with power and boldness. That same Spirit lives in us.

The Holy Spirit Is Not a Feeling But a Person

The Holy Spirit is not just a breeze or a burst of energy. He is the Third Person of the Trinity, fully God, sent into our hearts to sanctify, strengthen, and guide. He speaks quietly, convicts gently, comforts deeply.

He is the voice that reminds you, "You are not alone."
He is the fire that whispers, "Do not be afraid."

And He is the power that makes mercy possible - again and again.

The Gifts That Build Us

At Confirmation, we receive the seven gifts of the Holy Spirit, meant not only for our benefit, but for the building up of the Body of Christ:
- Wisdom - to see the world through God's eyes.
- Understanding - to grasp the truth of faith more deeply.
- Counsel (Right Judgment) - to choose rightly, especially when it is hard.
- Fortitude (Courage) - to endure suffering and stand firm in trials.
- Knowledge - to see God's hand in our lives.
- Piety (Reverence) - to love God with trust and affection.

- Fear of the Lord (Wonder and Awe) - to marvel at God's greatness and stay close to Him.

These are not just concepts. They are lived realities. They help us live with grace, forgive without resentment, stand up for what is right, and follow Christ even when it is costly.

The Fruits That Grow and Overflow

Where the Holy Spirit dwells, His fruits begin to grow. You might recognize them from Galatians 5:22–23: Love, joy, peace, patience, kindness, generosity, faithfulness, gentleness, self-control.

If these sound like the kind of person you long to be, take heart. The Spirit is already at work in you.

These are grown not by human effort. These fruits are not earned by striving harder. They come by remaining close to Christ. As Jesus said, "Remain in me… and you will bear much fruit." (John 15:5) And these gifts are for others, for their nourishment and to help them become disciples too.

Let The Spirit Lead

We cannot heal without the Holy Spirit. We cannot forgive without Him. We cannot walk into the sheepfold, or lead others there, without His help. We cannot have true community without Him. He is the breath in our lungs, the Advocate in our corner, the fire in our bones.

Invite Him daily. Trust Him deeply.
He will never abandon you.

Reflection Questions:
- When have I felt the quiet presence or prompting of the Holy Spirit?
- Which gifts of the Spirit do I need to ask for right now?
- Where is the Spirit bearing fruit in my life - and where do I need to surrender more?
- Read Acts of the Apostles 1:8, 2:1-13

49.   Walking With Virtue

> "Now these three remain: faith, hope, and love, but
> the greatest of these is love."
>
> – 1 Corinthians 13:13

If healing from wounds, betrayal and injustice is the clearing away of rubble, then virtue is what we build in its place. The Church teaches us that God does not just want us to survive - we are called to thrive. To become saints. And the road forward is paved with virtue.

The theological virtues and cardinal virtues are not abstract ideals, but real, tangible habits that form us, heal us, and empower us to live mercy with truth and strength. It is through these that we can truly be "Jesus with skin on" for others. And we have already seen them in action in working through the healing process!

The Theological Virtues: Gifts from God
These three virtues are infused in us at Baptism. We do not earn them. They are gifts, and they orient our hearts toward God.

Faith
Faith allows us to believe in God - and to trust in His promises, even when everything else seems to fall apart.

If you have been betrayed by someone who should have protected you, faith can feel risky. But slowly, gently, God invites you to trust Him - not because your suffering did not happen, but because He is the One who wants to heal you.

In this book, we have seen that faith is not blind. It is honest. It brings our wounds to the Lord and still whispers "I believe. Help my unbelief."

Hope
Hope believes that healing is possible. That God will keep His word. That even what was meant for evil can be turned into good.

Hope is the virtue that keeps us through our darkest days. It kept us praying even when we did not feel heard. It kept us working through resentment and grief. And it is the virtue that allows us to say, even today: My story is not over.

Charity (Love)

This is not the emotion of love - but the active choice to will the good of the other, even at great cost.

Love is what allows us to forgive - not to excuse sin, but to hand it to God. It is what enables us to speak truth - not to wound, but to protect.

It is the greatest virtue because it never ends. Love is what heaven is. And every act of love here on earth brings a little of heaven closer.

The Cardinal Virtues: Human Strength, Perfected by Grace

These four virtues are called "cardinal" because all other moral virtues hinge (the root meaning of *cardinal*) on them. They are like the muscles of the soul. The more we practice them, the stronger they get.

Prudence

Prudence helps us know the right thing to do in each situation. It does not rush. It listens. It discerns.

In this book, we have talked about holy boundaries, confrontation, and discernment. All of that is prudence in action. It is the virtue that helps us pause and pray: Lord, what do You want me to do?

Justice

Justice is giving others what is due to them - whether that's truth, respect, protection, or consequences.

True mercy, as we have explored, always includes justice. It names it. And it seeks to make things right, even when that is hard.

Fortitude

Fortitude is the courage to do what is right, even when it hurts.

Whether you are confronting an abuser, leaving a toxic environment, or choosing to forgive when your heart is not yet ready, fortitude carries you. It is not bravado. It is not aggression. It is perseverance in love.

Temperance

Temperance helps us master our desires so that they do not master us.

For many survivors of trauma, temperance means learning to regulate our emotions, desires, or impulses that try to fill the void. It teaches us

218

how to fast, how to rest, how to wait, how to speak - but also how to remain silent when needed.

Virtue Builds the Church
The virtues - especially when lived out in community - become the foundation of a healthy Church.
- Faith builds the Church on Christ.
- Hope sustains it through suffering and doubt.
- Love binds us together as one body in Christ.
- Prudence discerns how to thrive and make right decisions, even when difficult.
- Justice honors every person's dignity.
- Fortitude strengthens it to resist evil and do the right.
- Temperance keeps it pure and balanced.

We do not just need holy individuals. We need virtuous communities. And your healing journey is part of building one.

A Prayer for Virtue
Holy Spirit,
Strengthen in me what is weak.
Help me believe what I struggle to trust.
Help me hope when the world feels dark.
Teach me to love - not with words, but with action.
Form my mind in prudence,
My hands in justice,
My heart in courage,
My habits in temperance.
Shape me into the person You created me to be.
Amen.

For Reflection
- Which virtue feels strongest in my life right now? Which feels weakest?
- Have I ever seen a virtue lived out in a way that inspired me to heal or grow?
- What is one small step I can take to grow in one of these virtues this week?
- Read Galatians 5:22-23, 1 Corinthians 13:1-13

50. Living Mercy with Teeth

"Be merciful, just as your Father is merciful."

– Luke 6:36

True mercy is not a feeling. It is not merely a prayer whispered in quiet corners or a thought we carry in our hearts. True mercy moves, it acts. It takes on flesh. It shows up in kitchens, prisons, hospital rooms, and confessionals.

The Church, in her wisdom, teaches us how to put mercy into action through the Corporal and Spiritual Works of Mercy. These are not abstract ideals - they are concrete ways to love like Christ.

The Corporal Works of Mercy
These care for the body - the physical needs of our neighbor.
They are rooted in Matthew 25, where Jesus says, "Whatever you did for the least of these, you did for Me."
- Feed the hungry
- Give drink to the thirsty
- Clothe the naked
- Shelter the homeless
- Visit the sick
- Visit the imprisoned
- Bury the dead

These may seem ordinary, but they are sacred works of mercy. Every meal shared, every hospital visit, every coat given in the cold - it all carries eternal weight. Jesus hides Himself in those in need. And mercy serves Him there, even if we do not immediately recognize Him there.

The Spiritual Works of Mercy
These care for the soul. In some ways, they are harder - because they call for courage, discernment, and self-gift at a deeper level.
- Instruct the ignorant
- Counsel the doubtful
- Admonish the sinner
- Bear wrongs patiently
- Forgive offenses willingly
- Comfort the sorrowful
- Pray for the living and the dead

These are the works of mercy we perform when we listen without judgment, forgive when it hurts, and speak truth when silence would be easier. They often go unnoticed - but heaven sees.

Mercy Begins with the Wounded

If you have experienced trauma or deep wounds, you might wonder how these works of mercy apply to you. Maybe you do not feel strong enough to give much right now. Maybe you have spent years surviving rather than serving.

But mercy is not a burden - it is a gift. And it flows from healing. When we show mercy, we receive mercy.

You may find, as you heal, that you become a wellspring of mercy for others:
-   A listening ear for someone in pain.
-   A patient reminder for someone stuck in shame.
-   A quiet presence for someone who has no one left.

Even if you cannot do all seven works in either category, start with one. God does not expect us to pour from an empty cup - but He will fill us as we offer even the smallest act with love. And the more we authentically give, not out of force but of freedom, the more we are filled.

Mercy With Teeth - Through These Works

The works of mercy are not soft. They are strong. They require wisdom, boundaries, and courage.
-   Visiting the imprisoned does not mean endorsing injustice but recognizing the humanity of the incarcerated.
-   Admonishing the sinner does not mean condemning the soul but seeking for them to be reconciled to God.
-   Forgiving offenses does not mean tolerating abuse but about seeking to do what is right.

They require the kind of mercy that stands firm in truth and yet tender in love. Mercy with teeth.

For Reflection
- Which work of mercy - corporal or spiritual - do I feel most drawn to right now?
- Where in my life have I experienced one of these works done for me?
- How can I offer mercy to someone today, not in theory, but in action?
- Read Matthew 25:31-46, James 2:13

51. Before Moving On: To the One Who's Made It This Far

> I am confident of this, that the one who began a
> good work in you will continue to complete it until
> the day of Christ Jesus.

> – Philippians 1:6

If you are holding this book in your hands right now, and you have read every chapter - whether all at once, or in pieces through tears and courage - I want you to hear this clearly:

God sees you.

And you made it.

Not only through the pages.
- Through the pain.
- Through the doubts.
- Through the struggles.
- Through the lies.
- Through the voices that tried to keep you small.
- Through the systems that told you to sit down and be quiet.

You made it here. To this moment. To this breath.

And that is no small miracle.

Maybe you are still in the middle of the mess.

Maybe you are still sorting through the rubble.

Maybe you are only now realizing what was done to you - or what you survived.

That is okay.

Healing is not linear.

Grief is not predictable.

And faith, when it is honest, will sometimes look like wrestling (Genesis 32:25-29) more than resting (Hebrews 4:9-11).

You are not behind.
You are not broken beyond repair.
You are not walking alone.

Mercy with teeth helped you survive. And now, it will help you thrive.

This book was never meant to be an answer to all things.

It is a companion. A flashlight. A defiant reminder that evil does not get to win, silence does not get the final word, and shame does not get to tell your story.

Jesus does. And what a beautiful story He wants to tell in you!
And His voice is not one of guilt, gaslighting, or fear.

It is the voice of the Good Shepherd - calling you out of the valley, away from the wolves, protecting you from the thieves and hirelings, toward safety of the sheepfold, where you will find healing, truth, and life.

He wants you to live life abundantly. And when you are ready... even joyfully.

So take your time.
Keep going.
Keep naming.
Keep walking.
Keep hoping.
Keep showing mercy with teeth.

Because your story is sacred.
Your healing matters.
And the light still shines.

But the Lord desires more than your healing. He desires your heart to be united with His.
So together let us take that next step into something bigger.

52. The Sacrament of Being Home

> I am the living bread that came down from heaven;
> whoever eats this bread will live forever; and the
> bread that I will give is my flesh for the life of the
> world.
>
> – John 6:51

Throughout this journey, we have wrestled with sorrow, anger, memory, and healing. We have named wounds and explored the grace of mercy with strength. We have walked with saints and leaned into the arms of the Good Shepherd. But there is one place, one encounter, one gift that surpasses them all in both power and tenderness: the Eucharist.

The Eucharist is not a mere symbol or reminder. It is Jesus Christ - Body, Blood, Soul, and Divinity - fully present. In every celebration of the Mass, heaven meets earth. The Lamb of God, once slain, offers Himself again, not in suffering, but in sacrament. He invites us to communion - not only with Him, but with each other. In this sacred mystery, we receive not a piece of bread, but a Person. We receive love Himself.

And in this gift, we come home.

The Eucharist as Healing

The Eucharist is where our deepest wounds meet the Divine Physician. Christ does not wait for us to be whole before He gives Himself. He does not demand perfection before receiving us. He comes into our poverty, into our pain. Every Host is the One who bore our sins, carried our grief, and conquered death. In every chalice is the Blood that speaks louder than vengeance - the Blood that says, "You are forgiven. You are mine. You are loved."

Mass: The Communion of Heaven and Earth

At every Mass, we bring simple things - among the most ancient and universal of foods: bread and wine. But more than that, we bring ourselves: our joys and sorrows, our triumphs, and wounds. And in His mercy, He receives them all.

Through the hands of the priest, we hear again the words of the Last Supper:

"This is My Body... This is My Blood."

In that moment, bread and wine are no longer what they were. They become the true Body and Blood of Christ. It is the greatest exchange: we offer what is earthly, and God returns what is divine.

But what about us?
We, too, are transformed.
We become what we receive: the Body of Christ.
- Our suffering is met with His strength.
- Our sorrow is met with His comfort.
- Our joys are amplified by His delight.
- Our triumphs are crowned with His grace.

And reception of the Blessed Sacrament transforms us most powerfully. In the fourth century, St. John Chrysostom taught (emphasis mine):

> "He has given to those who desire Him not only to see Him, but even to touch, and eat Him, and fix their teeth in His flesh, and to embrace Him, and satisfy all their love. Let us then return from that table **like lions breathing fire**, having become terrible to the devil. "

> - St. John Chrysostom, Homily 46 on the Gospel of John (John 6)

Lions breathing fire! Talk about strength and confidence. Fearful to Satan, and if Satan, evil as well.

St. Augustine, in his Sermon 272 on the Eucharist, tells us we become what we receive. In these times we might say that we are what we eat. We receive the Body of Christ to become the Body of Christ, the Church. He instructs us to put ourselves into the paten, the plate or bowl that holds the hosts for consecration, and into the chalice, that is to become the Lord's Blood, in order to be transformed. This is true intimacy with God!

This happens at every single Mass - day after day, season after season. Because this is how He loves.
The Mass is where heaven and earth collide - not in destruction, but in glory.

It gives us a glimpse of eternity, a foretaste of our true home, and the strength to keep going.

So even if the music is not perfect, or the homily falls flat, or someone in the pew has wounded you - remember this:
You are not there for them.

You are there for Christ.
For the collision of heaven and earth.
For the Eucharist, where love is made visible.

Eucharistic Adoration: Home in His Presence

Even so, sometimes Mass might be too chaotic, or we might be too easily distracted, or we are too hurt that we are afraid. If that is the case, I offer this suggestion, seek a Church that offers adoration of the Blessed Sacrament, or at least opens the doors for the faithful to be in the Presence of Jesus Christ.

When we kneel in Adoration, we are not only praying to God - but we are also being with God. In the silence of the monstrance or tabernacle, there is no demand, no performance, no expectation. Only presence.

Adoration is the stillness of the prodigal son resting in the loving embrace of the Father. It is a sheep learning the voice of the Good Shepherd. It is St. John listening to the heart of the Savior. It is the gaze of the Blessed Mother at the foot of the cross. It is the whisper of Christ saying, "Abide in Me." Our best response might be the plea of the disciples on the road to Emmaus: "Stay with us, Lord..."

For those who have felt rejected, dismissed, unheard - Adoration is the radical welcome of the God who never left. He waits. Patiently. Quietly. Powerfully. Like a home with the door always open, the Eucharist is where we are seen, known, and loved - and where we are made whole.

A Final Invitation

If your journey has been hard, if forgiveness feels far, if healing is slow, come to the Eucharist. Come to the Altar, to the Tabernacle, to the chapel of Adoration. You do not need perfect words. You do not need to be already fixed or finished. You simply need to come willing to be healed and transformed.

There, in the mystery of Mercy made Flesh, is your home.

There, you will find the One who knows your wounds and offers His own in return.

There, in the Eucharist, Mercy bares its heart - not with violence, but with vulnerability. Not with teeth of violence, but of tenderness. And yet, still full of strength.

This is the home of healing.
This is the home of truth.
This is the home of Christ.
And He is waiting for you.

Lord Jesus, present in the Most Holy Sacrament,
You are the King of Peace and the Shepherd of the meek.
In Your silent strength and gentle presence,
teach me to be a builder of communion,
a vessel of Your peace,
and a disciple clothed in meekness and mercy.
Heal my divisions, calm my storms,
and train my heart to trust like Yours.
Let this time before You led me home to You.
Amen.

Reflection Questions
- What does it mean for me personally to "be home" with Jesus in the Eucharist? When have I experienced the Eucharist as a place of healing, safety, or return?
- How is the Lord inviting me to bring my wounds, grief, or struggles into His Eucharistic presence? What might I be holding back that needs to be surrendered in this sacred space?
- In what ways am I being called to become more Eucharistic in my daily life? Do I reflect Christ's self-giving love in how I live, forgive, and serve others?
- Read Luke 22:14-20, John 6

Postscript: A Follow Up

I began this book by sharing a painful episode involving my father. In the years that followed - though we had no direct contact - I saw him twice. The first was about two years later, after my sister's graduation program. I had to leave as quickly as I could. That was before I had truly entered the deeper work of healing.

Whenever I saw something that reminded me of him - or when I let my mind drift toward other wounds - resentment, anger, or pain would rise up, sometimes all at once. A wise spiritual director encouraged me to turn to the Lord, to acknowledge those feelings and offer them to Him in prayer, and to pray for my dad. I was invited to trust God with what I could not carry alone.

Then I began a particularly difficult pastoral assignment. I fell into unhealthy patterns - overworking, striving to meet unrealistic expectations, taking criticism too personally. I now see that I was responding not only to the pressures of ministry, but from the old wound. I started to feel depressed and sought help. Eventually, I reached a breaking point. I needed to step away in order to heal.

By God's mercy, I was given the opportunity to take time away. It was difficult, but in that safe place and time- working with a skilled psychologist - I confronted much of the trauma I had carried. The work was intense, but I found a sense of centeredness. For the first time in a long time, I felt like I was home.

When I returned, my bishop graciously gave me a year to serve as a parochial vicar. I was not a pastor but assisted another priest in his ministry as pastor. I knew I needed that time to rediscover the priesthood - not because I had lost it, but because I wanted to fall in love with it again. I wanted to serve from a place of freedom.

I then dove deep into books on spiritual warfare (as I felt I had been fighting a battle my entire life), healing, and boundaries. I took notes at first only to remind myself... and eventually to better serve others. Many of those notes and observations became this book.

After that year, I was assigned as a pastor. I am still serving - more in love with Christ, more in love with the Church and her people, more in love with life.

As I mentioned earlier, I saw my dad a second time. It was at my mother's funeral in 2022, a few years after my sabbatical. My father had told my sisters that he planned to attend and wanted to speak "to" me. I did not have the emotional strength to mourn the loss of my mother, lead my family in the funeral services, and engage in an unpredictable or painful conversation - no matter his intentions.

So, I wrote him a note. I explained that the day of my mother's funeral was not the time for any discussion. I asked that, if he still wished to talk, he could reach out in a few months. My sisters gave him the note, and a trusted friend stood nearby in case I needed support. My father respected the boundary. He never followed up.

All of this is to say: I am still healing.
But I am closer than I was yesterday - and certainly closer than when I first began.

Most days now, the hurt is little more than a small dull ache. Other days, it is more pronounced. Thankfully, those days are fewer and further between. And I have learned to be okay with both.

I may never understand why I cannot have a relationship with my father.
Maybe he is incapable.
Maybe he is unwilling to try.

But I know that I have tried.
And I release the pain, grief, sorrow, and any residual unforgiveness.
I will show him mercy -
mercy that holds on to the hope that God will make all things right.

I love my dad.
I forgive him.
I can honor him, but only in the manner that God desires.

I can accept that, for now, we cannot be in a reconciled relationship as father and son.
But I hope - by God's grace and mercy -
        that I will see him in eternity.

And I will laugh -

not that he made it,
but that God is so good.

And I will cry -
not in sadness for what was lost,
but in joy that for eternity, we can worship together.

I know that I no longer carry the wounds alone or in vain.
I know that they are carried and transformed in Christ.

And I do know this:
God is using my story.
And He is pleased with me.
He loves me - and always has.
All I need to do is stay close to Him,
and love Him in return.

If He can walk with me through fire,
I am certain He will walk with you.

Your story - like mine - is still being written.
And the Author is good.

Home (Closing Meditation)

Home is not a place -
a "where" of maps, locations, or points,
a destination or departure,
traveled to by planes or cars.

It is not a structure made for lodging,
a building constructed of wood or stone,
of mortar or brick.

There are no roofs or floors,
neither windows nor doors -
yet all are invited.

Home is a state of being,
an abiding in,
a being with -
not only where the heart dwells,
but where the heart and the Holy Spirit reside
in communion with each other.

Home is when joy overflows into tears and laughter,
when healing is found
in the Source of all being.

Home is love, mercy, forgiveness.

No, home is not a place -
but the enduring presence of our Lord.

Home is a "when":
when the Lord reveals His love,
His providence, His protection;
when all is right with the world
because peace is found in the soul.

Home may be a thousand miles from where we reside -
or it may be right where we are.

Home is a heart set free,
singing with the angels and saints -
a harmony the heart knows,
though the mind has yet to grasp it.

Home is found only by the soul longing to travel inward…
to find Him already waiting.

Appendix
A Note About Marriage, Separation, and Divorce

We cannot fight evil by choosing to do evil. Only God - and people who live by His gifts of the virtues, truth, justice, mercy, love, and forgiveness - can overcome it. It is never morally permissible to respond to sin with sin.

Still, some moral situations require careful discernment. For example, the Church opposes abortion-the direct and intentional taking of an unborn child's life. But Catholic moral theology includes the principle of double effect, which helps us understand how to navigate complex, life-threatening decisions. A classic case is an ectopic pregnancy, when a newly conceived child implants outside the womb, endangering both the child's and the mother's life. In such cases, a surgeon may intervene to save the mother, knowing the child will not survive. The loss of the child is not directly intended; it is a tragic but tolerated consequence of an act aimed at saving life - not taking it.

Similarly, we must pay attention to situations in marriage that cause serious harm. When one spouse refuses to live out the sacrament - through adultery, abuse, neglect, or other grave failures - the other spouse may, in good conscience, seek separation, at least temporarily, especially if reconciliation is not possible. In some cases, this separation may lead to civil divorce - not because the faithful spouse wishes to break the marriage, but because they must seek safety, justice, and healing.

Even Canon Law (Code of Canon Law §1151–1155) makes clear that a spouse is not morally obligated to remain in a situation of danger, abuse, or grave harm. The Church permits separation - and even civil divorce - provided it is not pursued with the intent to remarry unless a declaration of nullity is granted.

The Church presumes the validity of a sacramental marriage until proven otherwise. This is why, in cases of possible invalidity, the Church invites couples to bring their marriage before a tribunal, which may issue a declaration of nullity. Contrary to popular usage, this is not an "annulment" in the sense of canceling a marriage that once existed. Rather, it is a formal declaration that the sacrament never occurred, usually due to a defect of consent - meaning that one or both parties were incapable, at the time of the wedding, of truly entering into a sacramental bond (due to psychological immaturity, deception, addiction, or other grave impediments).

Even before such a declaration, separation or civil divorce may be morally permissible, especially when pursued not to escape a commitment, but to preserve one's dignity, safety, and relationship with God. The principle of double effect may help us understand that even though divorce is never the ideal outcome, it may be tolerated when the faithful spouse's intention is not to sever a sacrament, but to seek healing, truth, and protection.

This does not give permission to begin a new romantic relationship - even if it is chaste - unless and until the Church declares the marriage invalid. Until then, the faithful spouse must live as if the sacrament remains intact.

Marriage requires the willing participation of both spouses. When one refuses to work toward healing, reconciliation, or faithfulness, the other is not required to remain in a situation that endangers their physical, emotional, or spiritual well-being. Yes, the Church calls for better formation before marriage - but she also calls for better pastoral care during hardship.

The Church upholds the indissolubility of marriage, but she also upholds the dignity, safety, and holiness of her members. Sometimes, separation is not a betrayal of the sacrament, but an act of fidelity to what it was meant to be.

I know people who have agonized over the decision to separate - especially when children are involved. Some have come to realize that, to hold the other accountable, preserve their own capacity to love, or pursue reconciliation from a place of safety, separation was the only moral option. Many also pursue a declaration of nullity, and often, after prayerful examination, the Church recognizes that the sacrament never occurred. The reasons vary: an unwillingness to remain faithful, a refusal to share life fully, or serious psychological impairment, just to name a few.

I hate divorce. I have seen and experienced its pain firsthand - as a child of divorce, and as a pastor walking with families through it. It harms spouses, children, and the wider community. But that hatred does not blind me to reality. Abuse, adultery, spiritual neglect, and ongoing psychological harm are not lesser evils to divorce - they are grave sins. Sometimes, as Jesus said, "the greater sin" (John 19:11) belongs not to the one who walks away, but to the one who made doing so necessary.

Separation - even when it leads to divorce and a tribunal process - can be a courageous act of moral clarity, not a personal failure. It is often the "lesser evil," not chosen to destroy the sacrament, but to protect life, truth, and the possibility of healing.

When the Abuser Is a Priest or Religious

To be abused in any way is a terrible thing.

To be abused by someone who was supposed to be trustworthy - devoted to God - is even worse.

To be abused by a priest or religious, someone consecrated to Christ, is devastating.

These men and women made vows or promises - poverty or simplicity of life, chastity, and obedience. They were called to resist sin, protect the vulnerable, and live as signs of the Kingdom. They were supposed to be safe.

When they fail, the damage is extreme - to the survivor, to the Church, and to faith itself.
If this is your story:
> I am so sorry.

I am sorry for what was done to you. I am sorry for how it shattered your trust. I am sorry that someone who was supposed to represent Christ instead caused you harm.

And in the name of your abuser - though I have no right to speak for them - I apologize. Not to excuse the sin, but to affirm you: you never deserved that. Not as a person. Not as a parishioner. Not as a child of God.

You may have been dismissed when you tried to tell the truth.

You may have watched your abuser be reassigned, "treated," or described in vague euphemisms like boundary violation or moral failing, when you knew it was far worse.

You may have heard silence when you cried for justice.

And for that too: I am sorry.
And I know: that apology may feel like too little, too late.
I will not argue. But I offer it anyway - because you deserve to hear it.

When the Church Feels Like the Enemy

For many survivors, it is hard to separate what someone in the Church did from the Church itself. You may struggle with the phrase "the Church is holy" - how could something holy let this happen?

And yet, this is one of the painful paradoxes of our faith:
The Church is holy in her Head, Jesus Christ.
But she is also filled with sinners - including those who sinned against you.

And when a priest or religious betrays their vows, they do not just sin against you - they wound the Body of Christ itself.

You are not alone in your grief.
The Body of Christ is groaning for justice - even if you have not heard that cry in your parish.

A Long Pattern - a Long Path to Healing

Sadly, this is not a new wound. As far back as the 11th century, St. Peter Damian authored the Book of Gomorrah, warning against abuse in the clergy. He called for strong, merciful consequences - what we might call "mercy with teeth." Abusers were to live out their days in penance, always under supervision, never again alone, never again able to harm.

His call: immediate correction. Ongoing accountability. Never again.

We are still catching up to that wisdom.

Still, there are signs of hope. More Catholics are aware of the pain this has caused in so many survivors. More survivors are speaking. More people are listening to the stories and are actively watching and defending. While even one abuser is too many, you are no longer a lone voice in the wilderness. And your story may be part of the very renewal the Church so desperately needs.

Why Your Story Matters

Telling your story is an act of courage.
It cleanses. It warns. It invites others to speak.
It helps you heal, and it helps the Church face what she must.

So, thank you - for your courage.

240

Thank you for your honesty.
Thank you for not giving up.

And above all: do not give up on Jesus.
Do not abandon the Gospel because someone misused His name.
Do not give up on the Church - not for their sake, but for yours.

Christ still wants you to have an abundant life.
Christ is not your abuser.
Christ is the one who stood between the wolf and the sheep.
He still stands with you now.

Emotion Classification Chart

Sometimes, for the hurting, that terms of emotions are difficult. The following is chart that may help.

Primary Emotion	Secondary Emotions (More Specific Feelings)
Anger	Frustration, Irritation, Resentment, Rage, Envy, Jealousy, Hostility, Annoyance, Bitterness, Contempt, Disgust, Hatred, Exasperation
Sadness	Grief, Disappointment, Despair, Hopelessness, Loneliness, Shame, Guilt, Regret, Heartache, Hurt, Emptiness, Depression, Remorse, Ennui, Abandonment
Joy	Happiness, Contentment, Delight, Excitement, Gratitude, Pride (healthy), Love, Amusement, Hope, Optimism, Peace, Relief, Satisfaction, Awe
Fear	Anxiety, Worry, Panic, Insecurity, Dread, Nervousness, Terror, Alarm, Phobia, Apprehension, Helplessness
Love	Affection, Compassion, Trust, Intimacy, Caring, Devotion, Tenderness, Desire, Admiration, Attachment, Kindness
Surprise	Amazement, Shock, Disbelief, Confusion, Wonder, Awe, Intrigue
Disgust	Revulsion, Contempt, Rejection, Aversion
Shame/Guilt	Embarrassment, Humiliation, Self-loathing, Conscience-stricken

Resources
Praying With Scripture

> The Church "forcefully and specially exhorts all the Christian faithful . . . to learn 'the surpassing knowledge of Jesus Christ' (Phil 3:8) by frequent reading of the divine Scriptures... Let them remember, however, that prayer should accompany the reading of Sacred Scripture, so that a dialogue takes place between God and man. For 'we speak to him when we pray; we listen to him when we read the divine oracles.'"
>
> Catechism of the Catholic Church, ¶2653

The Church has long taught a particular method of praying with Scriptures (or the writings of the saints, for that matter in a lesser degree), It is called **Lectio Divina**. It consists of a few simple steps.

Statio - **(Station) Get to the Table**
Time – be consistent with length/time of day
Place – find a place with limited distractions. Put away cell phones, tv's, and music players. Perhaps setting a 'sacred space' with a religious image, a candle. Praying in front of the Blessed Sacrament is commendable, if possible.
Preparation – Find the passage. Prepare yourself by getting comfortable. Pray to the Holy Spirit while breathing slowly and deeply.
Lectio – **(Read) Take a bite.** Read the Scripture slowly and attentively 2-3 times, paying attention to the phrase or line that attracts your attention.
Meditatio – **(Meditation) Chew it.** Think about the portion that attracts you. Meditate and ruminate on it. Let the Spirit guide you and teach you.
Oratio – **(Prayer) Savor it.** Open your heart to God and pray to Him in a conversation.
Contemplatio – **(Contemplation) Digest it.** Focus on God, resting in His presence.
Collatio- **(Collation) Gather the leftovers.** Discuss what you have learned if done with others.
Actio- **(Action) Leave with the nourishment we have received.** Live what you have learned.

It is advised to begin with a prayer to the Holy Spirit, such as:
Come Holy Ghost, fill the hearts and minds of the faithful servants, and inflame them with the fire of Your divine love.

Let us pray: O God, who by the inspiration of the Holy Ghost, did instruct the hearts of Your faithful servants; grant us in the same Spirit, to discern what is right, and enjoy His comfort forever, through our Lord Jesus Christ, Who lives and reigns, one God, with You and the same Spirit, world without end. Amen.

(Note: A partial indulgence is granted to the faithful, who, under the usual conditions and with the veneration due the divine word, make a spiritual reading from Sacred Scripture. A plenary indulgence is granted under the usual conditions if this reading is continued for at least one half an hour.)

Closely related is a method of **Ignatian Contemplation**, a model given by St. Ignatius of Loyola, which engages the imagination. This method is appropriate for narratives, not necessarily for the Psalms or other writings.

1. **Find a gospel passage.** Short passages with characters and action work best.
2. **Ask the Holy Spirit for guidance.**
3. **Read the passage,** slowly and reflectively. Read it again, if needed.
4. **Begin imagining the scene** and interacting with it like a play in which you are an actor. Imagine the background, the props, the characters. Place yourself in one of the roles, such as a main character or an auxiliary character. Let the scene play out.
5. **Pay attention to your senses**- what do you smell, hear, taste, or touch (e.g., at the nativity, smell the straw, hear the animals, and hold the infant Jesus). Pay attention to the emotions that are stirring.
6. **Collect the prayer** - what lesson can you learn from this contemplation
7. **Close with an appropriate prayer and an Our Father**.

The following are some suggested readings for prayer when dealing with evil, seeking forgiveness, or in the process of repentance.
Psalm 3 - Trusting in the midst of enemies

Psalm 5 - Prayer for divine help
Psalm 6 - Prayer in distress
Psalm 7 - God the vindicator
Psalm 9 - Thanksgiving for victory
Psalm 10 - Prayer for vindication
Psalm 11 - Confidence in God
Psalm 12 - Prayer against evil tongues
Psalm 14 - Prayer in the midst of corruption
Psalm 17 - Prayer for rescue from persecutors
Psalm 22 - Prayer of an innocent person afflicted
Psalm 23 - The Lord is my Shepherd
Psalm 26 - Prayer of an innocent person
Psalm 32 - Prayer for remission of sin
Psalm 34 - Thanksgiving for God who rescues the just
Psalm 35 - Prayer for help against enemies
Psalm 36 - Wickedness and God's Providence
Psalm 37 - Fate of evildoers
Psalm 51 - Prayer for forgiveness
Psalm 52 - the deceitful tongue
Psalm 53 - Lament over corruption
Psalm 55 - Lament over betrayal
Psalm 56 - Trust in God in the midst of attack
Psalm 57 - Prayer for deliverance
Psalm 59 - Prayer against bloodthirsty enemies
Psalm 69 - Prayer in midst of great distress
Psalm 70 - Prayer for divine help
Psalm 73 - Trial of the just
Psalm 94 - Prayer for deliverance from wicked people
Psalm 102 - Prayer in time of distress
Psalm 109 - Prayer of one falsely accused
Psalm 130 - Prayer for pardon
Psalm 140 - Prayer for deliverance from the wicked
Psalm 141 - Prayer for deliverance from the wicked
Psalm 143 - Prayer in distress
Matthew 4:1-11, Luke 4:1-13 - The Temptation of Jesus
Matthew 5:1-12 - The beatitudes
Matthew 5:21-26 - Teaching on anger
Matthew 5:38-42 - Teaching on retaliation
Matthew 5:43-48, Luke 6:27-36 - love of enemies
Matthew 7:1-5, Luke 6:37-42 - Judging others
Matthew 10:16-25 - Coming Persecution

Matthew 10:26-33, Luke 12:2-9 - Courage in persecution
Matthew 11:25-30 - the gentle mastery of Christ
Matthew 13:24-30 - Weeds in wheat
Matthew 18:10-14, Luke 15:1-7 - Parable of the lost sheep
Matthew 18:21-35 - Parable of the unforgiving servant
Luke 1:46-55 - Mary's Magnificat
Luke 1:66:79 - Zechariah's Benedictus
Luke 3:1-18 - the preaching of John the Baptist
Luke 5:1-11 - the call of Simon the fisherman
Luke 5:27-32 - the call of Levi
Luke 7:36-50 - forgiveness of the woman caught in adultery
Luke 12:57-59 - settle with the opponent
Luke 15:8-10 - parable of the lost coin
Luke 15:11-31 - The prodigal son
Luke 19:1-10 - Zacchaeus the tax collector
John 10:11f - The Good Shepherd
John 15:1 17 - The vine and branches
Acts 15:1-20 - The Council of Jerusalem (conflict and resolution)
Ephesians 6:10-17 - the armor of God

Consciousness Examen

This is a prayer method to help one to become more aware of God's presence throughout the day. It is not about seeking forgiveness as the Examination of Conscience (discussed in the Chapter on the Sacrament of Reconciliation) but about becoming aware of God in the activity of the day by reflecting on where He was active with you. This is normally done at the end of the day, or several times throughout the day. The insight and graces you receive from this style of prayer confirm healing or demonstrate where the Lord wants to heal you.

Start with a prayer to the Holy Spirit to enlighten your mind and heart.
1. **Thanksgiving:** *Lord, I realize that all, even myself, is a gift from you.* Today, for what things am I most grateful?
2. **Intention:** *Lord, open my eyes and ears to be more honest with myself.* Today, what do I **really want** for myself?
3. **Examination:** *Lord, show me what has been happening to me and in me this day.* Today, in what ways have I experienced your love?
4. **Contrition:** *Lord, I am still learning to grow in your love.* Today, what choices have been inadequate responses to your love?
5. **Hope:** *Lord, let me look with longing toward the future.* Today, how will I let you lead me to a brighter tomorrow?

Prayers

Such a battle [against temptation] and such a victory become possible only through prayer. It is by his prayer that Jesus vanquishes the tempter, both at the outset of his public mission and in the ultimate struggle of his agony. In this petition to our heavenly Father [the Our Father's petition 'lead us not into temptation'], Christ unites us to his battle and his agony. He urges us to *vigilance* of the heart in communion with his own. Vigilance is "custody of the heart," and Jesus prayed for us to the Father: "Keep them in your name." The Holy Spirit constantly seeks to awaken us to keep watch. Finally, this petition takes on all its dramatic meaning in relation to the last temptation of our earthly battle; it asks for *final perseverance.* "Lo, I am coming like a thief! Blessed is he who is awake."

Catechism of the Catholic Church, ¶2849

Following are several written prayers that may be useful in your prayer. Sometimes, when we do not know how to pray, turning to prayers that are already written can help us find the words.

We remember, too, that prayer is communication with the Lord. That means listening as much as talking. Silence, therefore, is important. For those just beginning, silence is perhaps awkward, but necessary.

Prayer to St. Joseph, Just and Merciful

St. Joseph, Guardian of the Redeemer,
you were a man of justice and mercy, chosen to protect the Virgin and her Son - chosen to guard what was most holy in silence, strength, and love.
You did not speak many words, but your actions echoed into eternity.
When others would have exposed Mary to shame, you chose mercy.
When danger loomed, you listened to the voice of God and fled into the night.
When fear whispered, you stood firm in obedience.
When provision was needed, your hands gave faithfully.

St. Joseph, be a protector to me.
Intercede for me, that then Lord would:

    Shelter me from those that wound and hurt in word or deed,
    Recover what was lost or stolen from me,
    Help me choose mercy, even when I have been harmed.
    Strengthen me when the burden of forgiveness feels too heavy.

Please assist me by your prayers in the work I am to do,
Defend me against those that would fail to do theirs.
Stand beside me when justice is ignored.
Help me to learn by your example to trust in silence,
    to discern in stillness,
    to act not out of fear, but out of love.
Be near when I am tempted to despair.
Lift me up by your prayer when I am bent under the weight of sorrow.

You who kept watch over the Christ Child - keep watch over me.
You who were entrusted with Mary - intercede for all who are vulnerable.
You who led your family through exile and uncertainty – be my guide on my journey.

Intercede for me that I may believe that God can still bring life from what looks like death,
healing from hurt, and peace from pain.
And when I cannot find the words,
pray for me with your quiet strength.
St. Joseph, just and merciful, pray for us. Amen.
St. Joseph, just and merciful,

You chose the path of compassion over condemnation
And faith over fear.
By your example, teach us to be just and loving.
Help us to rise when God calls - quietly, obediently, and faithfully.
Ask your foster Son Jesus Christ to shape in us a heart like yours: firm, patient, and full of mercy.
Amen.

Litany of Healing

Lord Jesus,
You see what others ignored.
You hear what others silenced.
You repair the brokenhearted.
You do not look away from wounds.
You are mercy with tenderness and strength.
You are the Good Shepherd who lays down His life for the sheep -
not the hireling who runs,
not the thief that takes what is not his,
not the wolf who devours and destroys.
You came that we might have life, and have it abundantly.
Come and walk with us now.
Response: **Lord, in Your mercy, heal Your wounded ones.**

Response for the next section: **Deliver us, O Lord.**
From those who used Your name or teachings to control us,
From those that want no consequences of their injustice,
From silence that protected the powerful,
From the shame we were never meant to carry,
From the lie that we were to blame,
From the demand to be silent when suffering evil,
From 'reconciliation' demanded but not yet deserved,
From the fear of seeking justice for the vulnerable,
From the hesitance of telling the truth,

Response for the next section: **Grant us this grace, O Lord.**
For the courage to name what happened,
For strength to tell the truth,
For the wisdom to draw holy boundaries,
For holy anger that defends the innocent,
For the faith to believe our story is not over,
For the mercy to forgive,
For the justice to give mercy teeth.

When we were called divisive for speaking the truth,
Be our voice, O Lord.
When we were told to forgive and forget,
Be our clarity, O Lord.
When we were made to feel unsafe,
Be our refuge, O Lord.

When we felt unseen, unheard, and unloved,
Be our comfort, O Lord.
To those who are still in harm's way,
Be their protection, O Lord.
To those wrestling with anger and grief,
Be their peace, O Lord.
To those seeking to find You again,
Be their Shepherd, O Lord.
To those afraid to trust again,
Be their strength, O Lord.

Jesus, who cleansed the Temple -
Come and cleanse our hearts.
Jesus, who wept at the tomb of Lazarus -
Come and grieve with us.
Jesus, who forgave even when hearts were hard -
Come and walk with us into freedom.
Jesus, who laid down His life for the sheep -
Come and restore what was stolen
Jesus, who called out the wolves -
Come and give us mercy with teeth.
Jesus, who laid down His life to protect His own -
Come and strengthen us.
Jesus, who rose with wounds still visible -
Come, heal what still aches in us.

Lamb of God, who takes away the sins of the world,
Have mercy on us.
Lamb of God, who walks with the wounded,
Have mercy on us.
Lamb of God, who brings justice and healing,
Grant us Your peace.

Leader: You are the God who sees.
You are the Shepherd who does not abandon the flock.
You are the truth that sets us free.
All: **Bind up what was broken.**
Restore what was stolen.
Raise up what was dead.
Defend what is holy.
And lead us to healing. Amen.

Intercession of Saints of Mercy with Teeth
(Saints who lived truth and mercy with courage and conviction)

St. Joseph - Just, silent protector, father in mercy and courage
Pray for us...
Mary the Most Blessed Virgin - the mother of mercy and love
St. Peter - a man who tried so hard and sometimes failed, but never quit, and was our first pope
St. Paul - firm founder of community and preacher of the truth
St. James - who, like his brother St. John, had holy fire, but needed the Lord to temper it.
St. John, the Beloved - who loved the Lord, listened to His Sacred Heart, and stood in silent worship as our Lord was crucified
St. Monica - Model of persevering prayer and forgiveness
St. Augustine - Once wayward, became a bold voice of repentance and grace
St. Peter Damian - Reformer who boldly opposed clerical abuse and corruption
St. Joan of Arc - Obedient to God's call, martyred by political and ecclesial powers
St. Rita of Cascia - Wounded by vengeance, yet lived a life of healing and prayer
St. Thomas More - Martyr for conscience, faith, and truth over political pressure
St. Francis Xavier - Missionary with burning zeal for conversion and eternal life
St. Teresa of Avila - Mystic and reformer who faced resistance with holy fire
St. John of the Cross - Imprisoned by his brothers, yet wrote poetry of divine mercy
St. Francis de Sales - Conquered wrath with gentleness, preached truth in love
St. Catherine of Siena - Spoke boldly to popes, kings, and sinners alike
St. John Vianney - Spent much of his time in the confessional, leading many to repentance
St. Eugene de Mazenod - A son of divorce, he founded a community that served the abandoned
St. Damien of Molokai - Chose to live among lepers, died of their disease in love
St. Maria Goretti - Forgave her murderer from her deathbed

St. Edith Stein (Teresa Benedicta of the Cross) - Jewish convert, Carmelite, martyr at Auschwitz
St. Maximilian Kolbe - Offered his life for another in the face of evil
St. Josephine Bakhita - Enslaved, abused, yet found freedom and called herself "fortunate"
St. Oscar Romero - Assassinated for preaching justice and defending the poor
Bl. Stanley Rother - Refused to abandon his people in Guatemala; martyred in his rectory
Bl. Jerzy Popiełuszko - Polish priest-martyr who resisted communist oppression

All you saints of mercy with courage,
all you reformers and prophets,
all you wounded who chose healing,
all you faithful who spoke truth,
pray for us.
That we may live with courage,
love with justice,
forgive with truth,
and follow Christ with mercy that has teeth.
Amen.

(All proceeding prayers were by Fr. Todd Petersen)

Litany of Humility

Ascribed to Rafael Cardinal Merry del Val (1865-1930), Secretary of State for Pope Saint Pius X

O Jesus! meek and humble of heart, Hear me.
From the desire of being esteemed,   **Deliver me, Jesus.**
From the desire of being loved...
From the desire of being extolled ...
From the desire of being honored ...
From the desire of being praised ...
From the desire of being preferred to others...
From the desire of being consulted ...
From the desire of being approved ...
From the fear of being humiliated ...
From the fear of being despised...
From the fear of suffering rebukes ...
From the fear of being calumniated ...
From the fear of being forgotten ...
From the fear of being ridiculed ...
From the fear of being wronged ...
From the fear of being suspected ...

That others may be loved more than I, **Jesus, grant me the grace to desire it.**
That others may be esteemed more than I ...
That, in the opinion of the world,
others may increase and I may decrease ...
That others may be chosen and I set aside ...
That others may be praised and I unnoticed ...
That others may be preferred to me in everything...
That others may become holier than I, provided that I may become as holy as I should...

Litany of Divine Mercy

[The response to all invocations is, "**I Trust in You**."]

Divine Mercy, gushing forth from the bosom of the Father

Divine Mercy, greatest attribute of God

Divine Mercy, incomprehensible mystery

Divine Mercy, fountain gushing forth from the mystery of the Most Blessed Trinity

Divine Mercy, unfathomed by any intellect, human or angelic

Divine Mercy, from which wells forth all life and happiness

Divine Mercy, better than the heavens

Divine Mercy, source of miracles and wonders

Divine Mercy, encompassing the whole universe

Divine Mercy, descending to earth in the Person of the Incarnate Word

Divine Mercy, which flowed out from the open wound of the Heart of Jesus

Divine Mercy, enclosed in the Heart of Jesus for us, and especially for sinners

Divine Mercy, unfathomed in the institution of the Sacred Host

Divine Mercy, in the founding of the Holy Church

Divine Mercy, in the Sacrament of Holy Baptism

Divine Mercy, in our justification through Jesus Christ

Divine Mercy, accompanying us through our whole life

Divine Mercy, embracing us especially at the hour of death

Divine Mercy, endowing us with immortal life

Divine Mercy, accompanying us every moment of our life

Divine Mercy, shielding us from the fire of hell

Divine Mercy, in the conversion of hardened sinners

Divine Mercy, astonishment for Angels, incomprehensible to Saints

Divine Mercy, unfathomed in all the mysteries of God

Divine Mercy, lifting us out of every misery

Divine Mercy, source of our happiness and joy

Divine Mercy, in calling us forth from nothingness to existence

Divine Mercy, embracing all the works of His hands

Divine Mercy, crown of all God's handiwork

Divine Mercy, in which we are all immersed

Divine Mercy, sweet relief for anguished hearts

Divine Mercy, only hope of despairing souls

Divine Mercy, repose of hearts, peace amidst fear

Divine Mercy, delight and ecstasy of holy souls

Divine Mercy, inspiring hope against all hope

Concluding Prayer: Eternal God, in whom mercy is endless and the treasury of compassion inexhaustible, look kindly upon us and increase Your mercy in us, that in difficult moments we might not despair nor become despondent, but with great confidence submit ourselves to Your holy will, which is Love and Mercy itself.

[From the Diary of Sister Maria Faustina]

Litany of the Sacred Heart

Lord, Have Mercy on Us. **Lord, Have Mercy on Us.**
Christ, Have Mercy on Us. **Christ, Have Mercy on Us.**
Lord Have Mercy on Us. **Lord Have Mercy on Us.**
Jesus, Graciously Hear Us. **Jesus, Graciously Hear Us.**
God the Father of Heaven, **Have Mercy on Us.**
God the Son, Redeemer of the World, **Have Mercy on Us.**
God the Holy Ghost, **Have Mercy on Us.**

Sacred Head of Jesus, Formed by the Holy Ghost in the Womb of the Virgin Mary,
R to all: **Guide Us in All Our Ways**
Sacred Head of Jesus, Substantially United to the Word of God,
Sacred Head of Jesus, Temple of Divine Wisdom,
Sacred Head of Jesus, Center of Eternal Light,
Sacred Head of Jesus, Tabernacle of Divine Knowledge,
Sacred Head of Jesus, Safeguard Against Error,
Sacred Head of Jesus, Sunshine of Heaven and Earth,
Sacred Head of Jesus, Treasure of Science and Pledge of Faith,
Sacred Head of Jesus, Radiant with Beauty and Justice and Love,
Sacred Head of Jesus, Full of Grace and Truth,
Sacred Head of Jesus, Living Witness of Humility,
Sacred Head of Jesus, Reflecting the Infinite Majesty of God,
Sacred Head of Jesus, Center of the Universe,
Sacred Head of Jesus, Object of the Father's Joyous Satisfaction,
Sacred Head of Jesus, Upon Which the Holy Ghost Rested,
Sacred Head of Jesus, Around Which the Glory of Mt. Tabor Shown,
Sacred Head of Jesus, Who Had No Place on Earth on Which to Rest,
Sacred Head of Jesus, Whom the Fragrant Anointing of Magdalene Consoled,
Sacred Head of Jesus, Bathed with the Sweat of Blood in Gethsemane,
Sacred Head of Jesus, Who Wept for Our Sins,
Sacred Head of Jesus, Crowned with Thorns,
Sacred Head of Jesus, Outraged by the Indignities of the Passion,
Sacred Head of Jesus, Consoled by the Loving Gesture of Veronica,
Sacred Head of Jesus, Bowed to Earth Which was Redeemed at the Moment of Death on the Calvary,
Sacred Head of Jesus, Light of Every Being Born on Earth,
Sacred Head of Jesus, Our Guide and Our Hope,
Sacred Head of Jesus, Who Knows All Our Needs,
Sacred Head of Jesus, Who Gives Us All Graces,

Sacred Head of Jesus, That Governs All the Motions of the Sacred Heart,
Sacred Head of Jesus, whom we Wish to Adore and Make Known Throughout the World,
Sacred Head of Jesus, Who Knows All the Secrets of Our Hearts,
Sacred Head of Jesus, Who Enraptures Angels and the Saints,
Sacred Head of Jesus, Whom One Day We Hope to Behold Unveiled Forever,

Jesus, We Adore Your Sacred Head; We Surrender Utterly to All the Decrees of Your Infinite Wisdom.

Litany of Christ, High Priest and Victim

Lord, have mercy - **Lord, have mercy**
Christ have mercy - **Christ, have mercy**
Lord, have mercy - **Lord, have mercy**

Christ hear us - **Christ hear us**
Christ, graciously hear us - **Christ, graciously hear us**

God the Father of heaven, **Have mercy on us**
God the Son, Redeemer of the world,
God the Holy Spirit,
Holy Trinity, One God,

Jesus, Priest and Victim, **Have mercy on us**
Jesus, Priest forever according to the Order of Melchizedek,
Jesus, Priest Whom God sent to preach the Gospel to the poor,
Jesus, Priest Who at the Last Supper institute the form of the eternal sacrifice
Jesus, Priest Who lives forever to intercede for us,
Jesus, High Priest whom the Father anointed with the Holy Spirit and power,
Jesus, High Priest chosen from among men,
Jesus, made High Priest for men,
Jesus, High Priest of our confession of faith,
Jesus, High Priest of greater glory than Moses,
Jesus, High Priest of the true tabernacle,
Jesus, High Priest of the good things to come,
Jesus, High Priest, holy, innocent and undefiled,
Jesus, High Priest faithful and merciful,
Jesus, High Priest inflamed with zeal for God and souls,
Jesus, High Priest, perfect forever,
Jesus, High Priest, Who by Your own Blood entered the heavens,
Jesus, High Priest, who opened us a new way for us,
Jesus, High Priest, who loved us and washed us from our sins in Your Blood,
Jesus, High Priest, who offered Yourself to God as an oblation and sacrificial Victim,
Jesus, sacrificial Victim of God and men,
Jesus, holy and immaculate sacrificial Victim,
Jesus, pleasing sacrificial Victim,
Jesus, peace-making sacrificial Victim,

Jesus, sacrifice of propitiation and praise,
Jesus, sacrificial Victim of reconciliation and peace,
Jesus, sacrificial Victim in whom we have confidence and access to God,
Jesus, sacrificial Victim living forever and ever,

Be merciful, spare us, Jesus.
Be merciful, graciously hear us, Jesus.

From rashly entering the clergy, * **deliver us, Jesus**.
From the sin of sacrilege,
From the spirit of incontinence,
From sordid pursuits,
From every lapse into simony,
From the unworthy administration of the Church's treasures,
From the love of the world and its vanities,
From the unworthy celebration of Your Mysteries,
Through Your eternal priesthood,
Through the holy anointing whereby You were constituted a priest by God the Father,
Through Your priestly spirit,
Through that ministry whereby You glorified Your Father on earth,
Through the bloody immolation of Yourself made once and for all upon the Cross,
Through that same sacrifice daily renewed upon the altar,
Through that divine power which You exercise invisibly in Your priests,

That You would deign to maintain the whole priestly order in holy religion, * **We beseech You, hear us**
That You would deign to provide Your people with pastors after Your own heart,
That You would deign to fill them with the spirit of Your priesthood,
That the lips of Your priests might preserve true knowledge,
That You would deign to send faithful workers into Your harvest,
That You would deign to multiply the faithful dispensers of Your Mysteries,
That You would deign to grant them perseverance in the service of Your will,
That You would deign to give them gentleness in their ministry, resourcefulness in their actions, and constancy in prayer,
That through them You would deign to promote the veneration of the Blessed Sacrament everywhere,

That You would deign to receive into Your joy those who have served You well,

Lamb of God, Who take away the sin of the world, **spare us, O Lord**
Lamb of God, Who take away the sin of the world, **graciously hear us, O Lord**
Lamb of God, Who take away the sin of the world, **have mercy**

Jesus, Our Priest, **hear us**
Jesus, Our Priest, **graciously hear us**.

Let us pray:
O God, Sanctifier and Guardian of your Church, raise up in her through Your Spirit suitable and faithful dispensers of the holy Mysteries, so that by their ministry and example, the Christian people may be guided under Your protection in the path of salvation. Through Christ our Lord. Amen.

O God, who, while the disciples were worshiping and fasting, ordered Saul and Barnabas to be set apart for the work to which You had called them, be present now to Your Church in prayer, and You, who know the hearts of all, indicate those whom You have chosen for ministry. Through Christ our Lord. Amen.

(This prayer was prayed in Latin by Pope John Paul II as a seminarian in Cracow, and often in later life as well.)
Eccl. approval for English translation: - Adam Cardinal Maida, Archbishop of Detroit. Rescript of November 21, 2008

Litany of Loretto

Lord, have mercy.	**R: Lord, have mercy.**
Christ, have mercy.	**R: Christ, have mercy.**
Lord, have mercy.	**R: Lord, have mercy.**

Jesus, hear us.   **R: Jesus, graciously hear us.**
God, the Father of Heaven, **R: have mercy on us.**
God, the Son, Redeemer of the world,
God, the Holy Spirit,
Holy Trinity, One God,

Holy Mary,   **R: pray for us**
Holy Mother of God,
Holy Virgin of virgins,
Mother of Christ,
Mother of divine grace,
Mother most pure,
Mother most chaste,
Mother inviolate,
Mother undefiled,
Mother most amiable,
Mother most admirable,
Mother of good counsel,
Mother of our Creator,
Mother of our Savior,
Virgin most prudent,
Virgin most venerable,
Virgin most renowned,
Virgin most powerful,
Virgin most powerful,
Virgin most merciful,
Virgin most faithful,
Mirror of justice,
Seat of wisdom,
Cause of our joy,
Spiritual vessel,
Vessel of honor,
Singular vessel of devotion,
Mystical rose,
Tower of David,
Tower of ivory,

House of gold,
Ark of the covenant,
Gate of heaven,
Morning star,
Heath of the Sick,
Refuge of sinners,
Comforter of the afflicted,
Help of Christians,
Queen of Angels,
Queen of Patriarchs,
Queen of Prophets,
Queen of Apostles,
Queen of Martyrs,
Queen Confessors,
Queen of Virgins,
Queen of all Saints,
Queen conceived without original sin,
Queen assumed into heaven,
Queen of the most holy Rosary,
Queen of Peace,

Lamb of God, who take away the sins of the world, R: **spare us, O Lord,**
Lamb of God, who take away the sins of the world, R: **graciously hear us, O Lord.**
Lamb of God, who take away the sins of the world. R: **have mercy on us.**

Pray for us, O holy Mother of God.
R: That we may be made worthy of the promises of Christ.

Let us pray. Grant, we beg you, O Lord God, that we your servants, may enjoy lasting health of mind and body, and by the glorious intercession of the Blessed Mary, ever Virgin, be delivered from present sorrow and enter into the joy of eternal happiness. Through Christ our Lord. R: **Amen.**

Litany of Our Lady of Seven Sorrows
by Pope Pius VII

V. Lord, have mercy on us. **R. Christ, have mercy on us.**
V. Lord, have mercy on us. Christ, hear us. **R. Christ, graciously hear us.**

God, the Father of heaven, **R.: have mercy on us.**
God the Son, Redeemer of the world,
God the Holy Spirit,

Holy Mary, Mother of God, **R.: pray for us.**
Holy Virgin of virgins,
Mother of the Crucified,
Sorrowful Mother
Mournful Mother
Sighing Mother
Afflicted Mother
Forsaken Mother
Desolate Mother
Mother most sad
Mother set around with anguish
Mother overwhelmed by grief
Mother transfixed by a sword
Mother crucified in thy heart
Mother bereaved of thy Son
Sighing Dove
Mother of Dolors
Fount of tears
Sea of bitterness
Field of tribulation
Mass of suffering
Mirror of patience
Rock of constancy
Remedy in perplexity
Joy of the afflicted
Ark of the desolate
Refuge of the abandoned
Shield of the oppressed
Conqueror of the incredulous
Solace of the wretched

Medicine of the sick
Help of the faint
Strength of the weak
Protectress of those who fight
Haven of the shipwrecked
Calmer of tempests
Companion of the sorrowful
Retreat of those who groan
Terror of the treacherous
Standard-bearer of the Martyrs
Treasure of the Faithful
Light of Confessors
Pearl of Virgins
Comfort of Widows
Joy of all Saints
Queen of thy Servants
Holy Mary, who alone art unexampled

V. Pray for us, most Sorrowful Virgin,
R. That we may be made worthy of the promises of Christ.

Let us pray.
O God, in whose Passion, according to the prophecy of Simeon, a sword of grief pierced through the most sweet soul of Thy glorious Blessed Virgin Mother Mary: grant that we, who celebrate the memory of her Seven Sorrows, may obtain the happy effect of Thy Passion, Who lives and reigns world without end. Amen.

Litany of St. Joseph

Lord, have mercy.   R: **Lord, have mercy.**
Christ, have mercy.   R: **Christ, have mercy.**
Lord, have mercy.   R: **Lord, have mercy.**

Jesus hear us. R: **Jesus, graciously hear us.**
God, the Father of Heaven,   R: **have mercy on us.**
God, the Son, Redeemer of the world,
God, the Holy Spirit,
Holy Trinity, One God,

Holy Mary,   R: **pray for us.**
St. Joseph,
Renowned offspring of David,
Light of Patriarchs,
Spouse of the Mother of God,
Chaste guardian of the Virgin,
Foster father of the Son of God,
Diligent protector of Christ,
Head of the Holy Family,
Joseph most just,
Joseph most chaste,
Joseph most prudent,
Joseph most strong,
Joseph most obedient,
Joseph most faithful,
Mirror of patience,
Lover of poverty,
Model of artisans,
Glory of home life,
Guardian of virgins,
Pillar of families,
Solace of the wretched,
Hope of the sick,
Patron of the dying,
Terror of demons,
Protector of Holy Church,

Lamb of God, who take away the sins of the world, R: **spare us, O Lord.**

Lamb of God, who take away the sins of the world, R: **graciously hear us, O Lord.**

Lamb of God, who take away the sins of the world. R: **have mercy on us.**

He made him the lord of his household.   R: **And prince over all his possessions.**

Let us pray. O God, in your ineffable providence you were pleased to choose Blessed Joseph to be the spouse of your most holy Mother; grant, we beg you, that we may be worthy to have him for our intercessor in heaven whom on earth we venerate as our Protector: You who live and reign forever and ever. R: **Amen.**

The Rosary

The purpose of the Rosary is to help keep in memory certain principal events or mysteries in the history of our salvation, and to thank and praise God for them. There are twenty mysteries reflected upon in the Rosary, and these are divided into the Joyful, Luminous, Sorrowful, and Glorious Mysteries. It was embraced as a poor-man's psalter - those that could not read the 150 psalms (liturgically called the Psalter). The original 3 sets of mysteries (St. John Paul II added the Luminous mysteries) would have been 150 Hail Mary's - one for every Psalm.

The Sign of the Cross:

In the name of the Father, and of the Son, and of the Holy Spirit. Amen.

The Apostles' Creed:

I believe in God, the Father almighty, creator of heaven and earth. I believe in Jesus Christ, His only Son, our Lord. He was conceived by the power of the Holy Spirit and born of the Virgin Mary. He suffered under Pontius Pilate, was crucified, died, and was buried. He ascended into heaven, and is seated at the right hand of the Father. He will come to judge the living and the dead. I believe in the Holy Spirit, the holy Catholic Church, the communion of saints, the forgiveness of sins, the resurrection of the body, and life everlasting. Amen.

Our Father:

Our Father, who art in heaven, hallowed be thy name. Thy kingdom come, thy will be done, on earth as it is in heaven. Give us this day our daily bread, and forgive us our trespasses as we forgive those who trespass against us. Lead us not into temptation, but deliver us from evil. (For thine is the kingdom, and the power, and the glory now and forever.) Amen.

Hail Mary:

Hail Mary, full of grace, the Lord is with thee. Blessed are thou among women, and blest is the fruit of thy womb, Jesus. Holy Mary, Mother of God, pray for us sinners now, and at the hour of death. Amen.

Glory Be:

Glory be to the Father, and to the Son, and to the Holy Spirit, as it was in the beginning, is now, and forever will be forever, world without end. Amen.

O, My Jesus (Optional after Glory Be):
O My Jesus, forgive us our sins, save us from the fires of hell. Lead all souls to heaven, especially those most in need of thy mercy. Amen.

Hail, Holy Queen:
Hail, holy queen, mother of Mercy, our life, our sweetness, our hope. To thee do we cry, poor banished children of Eve. To thee do we send up our cries, mourning and weeping in this vale of tears. Turn, then, most gracious advocate, thine eyes of mercy on us, and after this our exile, show unto us the blessed fruit of thy womb, Jesus. O clement, O loving, O sweet Virgin Mary. Pray for us, holy Mother of God that we may be worthy of the promises of Christ.

Prayer after the Rosary:
O God, whose only begotten Son, by his life, death, and resurrection, has purchased for us the rewards of eternal life, grant, we beseech thee, that meditating upon these mysteries of the most holy rosary of the Blessed Virgin Mary, we may imitate what they contain, and obtain what they promise. Through the same Christ our Lord. Amen.

Memorare
Remember, O most gracious Virgin Mary, that never was it known that anyone who fled to thy protection, implored thy help, or sought thine intercession was left unaided.
Inspired by this confidence, I fly unto thee, O Virgin of virgins, my mother; to thee do I come, before thee I stand, sinful and sorrowful. O Mother of the Word Incarnate, despise not my petitions, but in thy mercy hear and answer me. Amen.

The Format of the Holy Rosary:
The Sign of the Cross and the Creed
The Our Father
3 "Hail Mary's
Glory Be
The mystery is announced, then the Our Father
10 Hail Mary's,
1 Glory Be and Optional "O my Jesus"
The mystery is announced, the Our Father (repeat for all mysteries)
When back to Center, pray the "Hail, Holy Queen" and concluding prayer

The Joyful Mysteries:
(Monday and Saturday, Sundays of Christmas)
The Annunciation - Humility
The Visitation - Love of Neighbor
The Nativity - Poverty of Spirit
The Presentation in the Temple - Purity of mind and body
The Finding of Jesus in the Temple - Obedience

The Luminous Mysteries:
(As invited By Pope John Paul II - Thursday)
The Baptism of the Lord- Spiritual Fruit: Sacrament of Baptism
The Wedding at Cana- Spiritual Fruit: Fidelity
The Proclamation of the Kingdom- Spiritual Fruit: Desire for Holiness
The Transfiguration- Spiritual Fruit: Spiritual Courage
The Institution of the Eucharist- Spiritual Fruit: Love of our Eucharistic Lord

The Sorrowful Mysteries:
(Tuesday and Friday, and Sundays of Lent)
The Agony in the Garden - God's Will be done
The Scourging at the Pillar - Mortification of the senses
The Crowning with Thorns - Reign of Christ in our heart
The Carrying of the Cross - Patient bearing of trials
The Crucifixion - Pardoning of Injuries

The Glorious Mysteries:
(Wednesday and Sunday outside Lent and Christmas)
The Resurrection - Faith
The Ascension - Christian Hope
The Descent of the Holy Spirit - Gifts of the Holy Spirit
The Assumption of the Blessed Mother - To Jesus through Mary
The Coronation of the Blessed Mother - Grace of Final Perseverance

Chaplet of Divine Mercy

1. Make the Sign of the Cross
In the name of the Father, and of the Son, and of the Holy Spirit. Amen.

2. Optional Opening Prayers
You expired, Jesus, but the source of life gushed forth for souls, and the ocean of mercy opened up for the whole world. O Fount of Life, unfathomable Divine Mercy, envelop the whole world and empty Yourself out upon us.

(Repeat three times)
O Blood and Water, which gushed forth from the Heart of Jesus as a fount of mercy for us, I trust in You!

3. Our Father
Our Father, Who art in heaven, hallowed be Thy name; Thy kingdom come; Thy will be done on earth as it is in heaven. Give us this day our daily bread; and forgive us our trespasses as we forgive those who trespass against us; and lead us not into temptation, but deliver us from evil, Amen.

4. Hail Mary
Hail Mary, full of grace. The Lord is with thee. Blessed art thou amongst women, and blessed is the fruit of thy womb, Jesus. Holy Mary, Mother of God, pray for us sinners, now and at the hour of our death, Amen.

5. The Apostles' Creed
I believe in God, the Father almighty, Creator of heaven and earth, and in Jesus Christ, His only Son, our Lord, who was conceived by the Holy Spirit, born of the Virgin Mary, suffered under Pontius Pilate, was crucified, died and was buried; He descended into hell; on the third day He rose again from the dead; He ascended into heaven, and is seated at the right hand of God the Father almighty; from there He will come to judge the living and the dead. I believe in the Holy Spirit, the holy Catholic Church, the communion of saints, the forgiveness of sins, the resurrection of the body, and life everlasting. Amen.

6. The Eternal Father
Eternal Father, I offer you the Body and Blood, Soul and Divinity of Your Dearly Beloved Son, Our Lord, Jesus Christ, in atonement for our sins and those of the whole world.

7. On the 10 Small Beads of Each Decade
For the sake of His sorrowful Passion, have mercy on us and on the whole world.

8. Repeat for the remaining decades
Saying the "Eternal Father" (6) on the "Our Father" bead and then 10 "For the sake of His sorrowful Passion" (7) on the following "Hail Mary" beads.

9. Conclude with Holy God (Repeat three times)
Holy God, Holy Mighty One, Holy Immortal One, have mercy on us and on the whole world.

10. Optional Closing Prayer
Eternal God, in whom mercy is endless and the treasury of compassion - inexhaustible, look kindly upon us and increase Your mercy in us, that in difficult moments we might not despair nor become despondent, but with great confidence submit ourselves to Your holy will, which is Love and Mercy itself.

Sub Tuum Praesidium
Beneath your compassion,
We take refuge, O Theotokos [*God-bearer*]:
do not despise our petitions in time of trouble:
but rescue us from dangers,
only pure, only blessed one.

Binding Prayers
Fr. Chad Rippenger has written or collated a number of powerful prayers. See his website (sensustraditionis.org) for links and explanations.

Suggested reading

For a Psychological perspective

- **Boundaries: When to Say Yes, How to Say No to Take Control of Your Life** Henry Cloud and John Townsend, Zondervan (1992). This foundational work launched the popular Boundaries series. It has been updated.
- **Boundaries in Marriage: Understanding the Choices That Make or Break Loving Relationships** Henry Cloud and John Townsend, Zondervan (1999)
- **Boundaries in Dating: How Healthy Choices Grow Healthy Relationships** Henry Cloud and John Townsend, Zondervan (2000)
- **Boundaries with Kids: How Healthy Choices Grow Healthy Children** Henry Cloud and John Townsend, Zondervan (1998)
- **Safe People: How to Find Relationships That Are Good for You and Avoid Those That Aren't** Henry Cloud and John Townsend, Zondervan (1995)
- **Changes That Heal: How to Understand the Past to Ensure a Healthier Future** Henry Cloud, Thomas Nelson (1992)
- **Integrity: The Courage to Meet the Demands of Reality** Henry Cloud, HarperBusiness (2006)
- **How People Grow: What the Bible Reveals About Personal Growth** Henry Cloud and John Townsend, Zondervan (2001)
- **Necessary Endings: The Employees, Businesses, and Relationships That All of Us Have to Give Up in Order to Move Forward** Henry Cloud, Simon & Schuster (2011)
- **Boundaries for Leaders: Results, Relationships, and Being Ridiculously in Charge** Henry Cloud, HarperBusiness (2013)
- **The Power of the Other: The startling effect other people have on you...** Henry Cloud, HarperBusiness (2016)
- **Never Go Back: 10 Things You'll Never Do Again** Henry Cloud, Zondervan (2014)
- **Trust: Knowing When to Give It, When to Withhold It, How to Earn It...** Henry Cloud, Simon & Schuster (2023)
- **Born Only Once: The Miracle of Affirmation** Conrad Baars, Franciscan Herald Press, 1975 (original edition), Wipf & Stock, 2016 (3rd edition)
- **Feeling and Healing Your Emotions** Conrad Baars, Logos Associates, 1979 (original edition), Bridge-Logos, 2003 (reprint)

- **Healing the Unaffirmed: Recognizing Emotional Deprivation Disorder** Conrad Baars and Co-author: Anna A. Terruwe Alba House 1976 (original) 2002 (revised edition)
- **Psychic Wholeness and Healing: Using All the Powers of the Human Psyche** Conrad Baars and Co-author: Anna A. Terruwe Alba House, 1981

Wounds/healing

- **A Father Who Keeps His Promise** - Scott Hahn (Servant Books/Dynamic Catholic)
- **The Healing Power of a Father's Blessing** - Linda Schubert (Miracles of the Heart Ministries)
- **True Confessions**– Linda Schubert (Miracles of the Heart Ministries)
- **Letter to a Suffering Church**– Bishop Robert Barron (Word on Fire)
- **Abba's Heart**– Linda Schubert (Miracles of the Heart Ministries)
- **When to Walk Away**– Gary Thomas (Zondervan)
- **Healing From Abuse**– Shannon Thomas, LCSW (Mast Publishing House)
- **Man's Search for Meaning**– Viktor Frankl (Beacon Press)
- **Yes to Life - In Spite of Everything**– Viktor Frankl (Beacon Press)
- **Overcoming Sinful Anger**– Fr. T.G. Morrow (Sophia Institute Press)
- **Be Healed: A Guide to Encountering the Powerful Love of Jesus in Your Life**– Dr. Bob Schuchts, Ave Maria Press, 2014 (paperback & hardcover editions)
- **Be Transformed: The Healing Power of the Sacraments**– Dr. Bob Schuchts, Ave Maria Press, (follow-up to Be Healed)
- **Be Restored: Healing Our Sexual Wounds through Jesus' Merciful Love**– Dr. Bob Schuchts, Ave Maria Press, (date circa 2019)
- **Be Devoted: Restoring Friendship, Passion, and Communion in Your Marriage**– Dr. Bob Schuchts, Ave Maria Press, 2020
- **Do You Want to Be Healed?: A 10-Day Scriptural Retreat with Jesus**– Dr. Bob Schuchts, Ave Maria Press, 2022
- **Real Suffering: Finding Hope and Healing in the Trials of Life**– Dr. Bob Schuchts, Ave Maria Press (approx. 2021)

Spiritual Warfare

- **Spiritual Warfare and the Discernment of Spirits–** Dan Burke, Sophia Institute Press
- **Unbound–** A Practical Guide to Deliverance Neil Lozano, Chosen
- **Resisting the Devil–** Neal Lozano, Our Sunday Visitor
- **Slaying Dragons– What Exorcists See & What We Should Know** Charles D. Fraune Slaying Dragons Press
- **The Rise of the Occult–** Charles D. Fraune, Slaying Dragons Press
- **The Occult Among Us–** Charles D. Fraune, Slaying Dragons Press
- **Exorcism - The Battle against Satan and His Demons–** Fr. Vincent Lampert, Emmaus Road Publishing
- **The Spiritual Combat–** Lorenzo Scupoli, Tan Classics
  - A 16th Century work, a reminder that spiritual perfection is a battle for our souls

Index

harm, 3, 6, 10, 19, 25, 26, 41,
44, 45, 47, 52, 65, 78, 84, 90,
93, 95, 97, 98, 99, 107, 108,
109, 117, 135, 136, 137, 145,
155, 156, 162, 167, 169, 235,
236, 237, 240
healing, 3, 12, 21, 24, 26, 27,
30, 35, 36, 41, 45, 49, 54, 56,
57, 58, 61, 63, 65, 66, 67, 72,
75, 76, 78, 79, 81, 83, 84, 86,
89, 90, 91, 93, 94, 95, 96, 98,
99, 100, 103, 104, 105, 106,
110, 123, 124, 125, 126, 127,
128, 131, 135, 136, 144, 145,
147, 148, 149,151, 152, 154,
156, 157, 159, 161, 165, 167,
171, 173, 175, 176, 178, 180,
183, 184, 185, 186, 208, 209,
213, 225, 226, 229, 235, 236,
237, 240
hireling, 37, 38, 39, 47, 48, 49,
50, 51, 52, 145, 166, 183, 226
hurt, 1, 3, 4, 23, 26, 27, 35, 43,
49, 56, 66, 72, 78, 85, 86, 87,
91, 94, 96, 99, 100, 103, 106,
108, 127, 133, 136, 145, 160,
167, 185, 186, 201
identity, 35, 43, 46, 93, 100
Jesus Christ, 3, 4, 9, 12, 13, 15,
16, 21, 24, 25, 26, 29, 30, 32,
33, 34, 35, 37, 39, 40, 41, 43,
44, 45, 46, 47, 49, 50, 51, 53,
56, 57, 58, 59, 60, 86, 89, 90,
91, 93, 94, 98, 99, 100, 104,
105, 109, 110, 113, 114, 116,
118, 119, 122, 123, 124, 126,
128, 132, 133, 153, 159, 160,
161, 162, 186, 189, 190, 193,
194, 195, 198, 204, 205, 208,
209, 211, 212, 213, 214, 226,
227, 228, 229, 237

justice, 3, 4, 7, 9, 10, 19, 21,
25, 59, 60, 61, 62, 66, 86, 99,
101, 103, 105, 106, 107, 108,
109, 110, 111, 115, 123, 127,
131, 132, 133, 135, 136, 137,
142, 147, 149, 154, 179, 193,
197, 198, 199, 202, 204, 205,
212, 213, 217, 218, 222, 235
lust of the eyes, 11, 20, 21
lust of the flesh, 11, 20, 21
manipulation, 19, 26, 31, 40,
44, 45, 51, 52, 61, 76, 79, 85,
86, 90, 114, 119, 125, 126, 131,
139, 148, 160, 165
marriage, 160, 167, 208, 213,
235, 236
mercy, 3, 4, 9, 14, 15, 21, 25,
35, 41, 53, 55, 90, 96, 99, 104,
106, 107, 108, 109, 110, 111,
112, 113, 114, 115, 117, 139,
140, 190, 193, 194, 196, 197,
199, 201, 204, 205, 208, 209,
212, 214, 215, 221, 222, 227,
230, 235
mercy with teeth, 4, 16, 72, 76,
99, 104, 109, 111, 112, 114,
117, 142, 160, 170, 226, 232,
240
name, 4, 23, 25, 26, 30, 33, 36,
37, 39, 44, 45, 52, 53, 60, 62,
63, 66, 67, 72, 76, 82, 83, 85,
86, 87, 88, 94, 95, 103, 109,
126, 127, 133, 136, 156, 175,
211, 226, 227
power, 3, 20, 21, 33, 34, 35, 40,
49, 52, 85, 88, 96, 145, 152,
160, 162, 211, 212, 214, 227
predator, 47, 51, 52, 53, 113
pride, 6, 11, 20, 21, 30, 44, 78,
119, 179, 193, 214
pride of life, 11, 20, 21

About the Author

Fr. Todd J. Petersen is a Catholic priest of the Diocese of New Ulm, Minnesota. The second of four children and the son of a divorced couple, he understands firsthand the complexities of family life and the need for healing.

He holds a Master of Divinity (M.Div.) and a Master of Arts in Theology (MAT) with a focus on Sacred Scripture from the St. Paul Seminary School of Divinity in St. Paul, Minnesota.

Ordained in 1999, Fr. Petersen has served in multiple parishes and ministered for 12 years as Director of the Office of Vocations for the Diocese of New Ulm.

As a fellow traveler on the journey to healing, he hopes this book will bring readers hope, freedom, and deeper union with Christ.

www.MercyWithTeeth.com

MERCY WITH TEETH
— PRESS —

www.ingramcontent.com/pod-product-compliance
Lightning Source LLC
Chambersburg PA
CBHW021709120626
46545CB00004B/1473